Writing a Legal Memo

by

John Bronsteen
Assistant Professor
Loyola University Chicago
School of Law

FOUNDATION PRESS
2006

This publication was created to provide you with accurate and authoritative information concerning the subject matter covered; however, this publication was not necessarily prepared by persons licensed to practice law in a particular jurisdiction. The publisher is not engaged in rendering legal or other professional advice and this publication is not a substitute for the advice of an attorney. If you require legal or other expert advice, you should seek the services of a competent attorney or other professional.

Nothing contained herein is intended or written to be used for the purposes of 1) avoiding penalties imposed under the federal Internal Revenue Code, or 2) promoting, marketing or recommending to another party any transaction or matter addressed herein.

© 2006 By FOUNDATION PRESS
          395 Hudson Street
          New York, NY 10014
          Phone Toll Free 1–877–888–1330
          Fax (212) 367–6799
          foundation–press.com
Printed in the United States of America

ISBN–13: 978–1–59941–002–9
ISBN–10: 1–59941–002–8

For my parents and sister

Acknowledgments

I am greatly indebted to the people who helped me produce this book.

The first is Melanie Miles, whose invaluable research assistance made my task manageable. I can't thank her enough.

Then there are Scott Chesin and Jonathan Masur, whose editing was both impeccable and immediate. Their selfless efforts bring to mind the words of William Butler Yeats: "Think where man's glory most begins and ends, / And say my glory was I had such friends."

Finally, I owe everything I know about legal writing to Rob Harrison. It's an honor to pass on to others the fruits of his remarkable teaching.

Contents

Writing a Legal Memo

INTRODUCTION

When you start out as a lawyer, your boss might well give you an assignment like this one: *"Here's a legal question. Find out the answer and tell it to me in a memo."* There's a good chance you'll hear such a request no matter where you decide to work—a law firm, a public interest organization, a government post, or a judicial clerkship. This book teaches you how to do that assignment: how to find an answer, and how to convey it in the form of a memo.

You find an answer by doing legal research—looking up the cases, statutes, and other sources that tell you what the law says about the topic you've been given. Over the past two hundred years, American courts have created an ocean of law by deciding millions of cases. That body of law can be hard to navigate, but fortunately there are sophisticated legal research tools to help you. When we get to Chapter 4, I'll describe how to use those tools.

Once you've found the answer, you need to write an essay explaining it. The best essays usually follow a certain format specific to legal memos. The format involves breaking up the essay into sub-issues and, within each sub-issue, describing the law before applying it to the facts of your case. Although the essay will be the main part of your memo, it won't be the only part; you'll also summarize the essay's key points in various other sections of the memo. In Chapter 3, I explain how to write both the essay and the other sections.

Why aren't those the only two chapters of the book? Chapter 4 tells you how to find your answer, and Chapter 3 tells you how to put it into the form of a memo, so what else is there?

You need to learn some background information in order for Chapters 3 and 4 to make sense. First, legal research is impossible without an understanding of how the American legal system works. You have to know which courts' decisions are most relevant to your question and how court decisions interact with statutes and with other sources of law. And there are points to learn that are more basic still—for example, what a statute *is*. I describe the American legal system in Chapter 1.

Second, it does you no good to use the proper format for a memo if the sentences you fill it with are unclear and poorly written. Most legal writing is hard to read, and although everyone laments this fact, few take tangible steps to fix it. If you follow a couple of simple rules, your sentences will make it easy for a reader to understand the information you're trying to get across. I outline those rules in Chapter 2.

Some helpful miscellaneous tips don't fit neatly into any of the first four chapters, so I present them in Chapter 5.

Finally, writing a legal memo requires you to know how to cite legal authority. In your memo, whenever you explain what the law says, you're expected to supply a citation that shows where you got your information and enables the reader to check it. There are hundreds of rules for how to do this, all contained in a book called *The Bluebook: A Uniform System of Citation*. I try to make your task easier by summarizing the most important rules in Chapter 6.

Because it would be unwieldy to reread this book whenever you need to write a memo, Chapter 7 gives you a checklist of the most important points. It should be a handy reference.

It's worth mentioning why the chapter on clear sentences comes so early in the book, before everything except the introduction to the legal system. One reason is that most legal writing courses start with assignments that require only writing and no research, then build toward assignments that involve both. You'll be expected to write clear sentences for the early assignments, so it makes sense to learn first how to do that.

The other reason I've put the chapter on clear sentences so early is that I want to increase the odds you'll read it. Legal research, memo formatting, and *The Bluebook* are foreign to most non-lawyers, so everyone realizes the necessity of learning about those things. By contrast, no one gets to law school without having written many sentences; and few people see the need to change the way they write. That's a shame, because one or two easy adjustments in your approach to writing a sentence

3

can turn a good writer into a great one, or a bad writer into a good one. If you give my suggestions a chance, you'll do a great service to your readers.

Before we get to the writing principles, we need to make a quick detour through the workings of the legal system.

Chapter 1

THE AMERICAN LEGAL SYSTEM

You've probably heard that the U.S. government has three branches (legislative, executive, and judicial), and that the branches respectively write, enforce, and interpret the laws. You've heard of Congress, the President, and the Supreme Court; and you might even be aware that there's a difference between federal and state governments.

But do you understand how the laws really work? Does the President (who heads the executive branch) personally enforce the laws that Congress passes? What does it mean to enforce a law, anyway? How do the three branches really interact, and how do state governments interact with the federal government? Which courts have to follow the decisions of which other courts?

I'll try to answer these and other questions in this chapter, spelling out how the system of American law is arranged.

I.   The Structure of the Government

The first thing you need to know is rather startling: There are fifty-two separate governments within the United States.[1] Each of the fifty states, plus the District of Columbia, has its own *state* government; and there is also a national (or *federal*) government that makes laws affecting people in every state.

Let's first see what the federal government looks like, then move on to the state governments (which are very similar to their federal counterpart).

A. The Federal Government: Three Branches

At the top of the federal government sits not a person but a piece of paper—the U.S. Constitution. Written in 1787 and ratified in 1789, the Constitution created the federal government. It divided federal power into three branches: the legislative branch (which creates laws), the executive branch (which enforces laws), and the judicial branch (which resolves disputes about the meaning of laws).

The legislative branch includes only one thing, the U.S. Congress, which is itself divided into a Senate and a House of Representatives. When a majority of Senators and a majority of Representatives vote in favor of a proposal (a bill), and the President signs it, then that bill becomes a federal law and applies to everyone in the country.

[1] This excludes local governments (e.g., city governments), for the sake of simplicity.

The executive branch is headed by the U.S. President. The President appoints the heads of federal agencies like the Federal Bureau of Investigation (FBI—the federal police force), and those agencies make sure that people obey the laws passed by Congress.

The judicial branch is headed by the U.S. Supreme Court and also includes the federal courts of appeals and the federal trial courts.

All of this will be fleshed out in a moment by some examples and a chart, but first let's glance at the state governments.

B. The State Governments: Three Branches

Each of the fifty states has its own state constitution, which creates a state government with a three-branch structure similar to that of the federal government. Thus, each state has:

(1) its own state legislature (typically composed of a state senate and a state house of representatives),[2] which creates laws;

(2) its own state executive branch (headed by the state's governor and also including state agencies like the state police force), which makes sure that people obey the laws passed by the state legislature; and

[2] Only Nebraska has a state legislature composed of one unitary body rather than a separate senate and house.

(3) its own state judicial branch (typically including a state supreme court, along with state trial courts and state courts of appeals).[3]

C.   Chart

Federal Government

U.S. Constitution

Legislative Branch	Executive Branch	Judicial Branch
• Congress (Senate, House)	1. President 2. Agencies (FBI, DOJ, DOT, EPA, FCC, etc.)[4]	1. Supreme Court 2. Federal courts of appeals 3. Federal district courts

State Governments

State Constitution

Legislative Branch	Executive Branch	Judicial Branch
• State legislature (Senate, House)	1. Governor 2. Agencies (police, prosecutors, regulators)	1. State highest court 2. State courts of appeals 3. State trial courts

[3] Some states have only two levels of courts—trial courts and a supreme court.

[4] These acronyms stand for the Federal Bureau of Investigation, the Department of Justice, the Department of Transportation, the Environmental Protection Agency, and the Federal Communications Commission.

D. An Example

To see how this legal structure works in practice, let's look at an example. Imagine that members of the Ku Klux Klan start harassing and intimidating minority groups in a state. The state legislature might respond by writing a bill that says anyone who engages in such activities will have committed a crime and will be sentenced to at least five years in prison. Once a majority of the state senate and a majority of the state house of representatives have voted for the bill, and the governor has signed it, the bill becomes a state law. Suppose the KKK members ignore the law and continue their harassment. Now the state police, who work for the governor (in the state executive branch, which enforces the laws created by the state legislature), will track down and arrest the people who have broken the law. Those offenders will then go to state trial court, where they will be prosecuted by state lawyers who (as part of the state executive branch) help the police enforce the laws passed by the legislature. If the jury in the state trial court finds the KKK members guilty, then they will be sent to state prison for at least five years.

What if the state legislature hadn't passed a law banning the harassment, or what if the state executive branch had chosen not to arrest and prosecute the offenders? The federal legislature (the U.S. Congress) could have created an identical law, by a majority vote of both the U.S. Senate and the U.S. House of Representatives and the signature of

9

the U.S. President.[5] Then, if the KKK members broke the law, the FBI (the federal police, who work for the President in the federal executive branch to enforce laws passed by the federal legislature) would travel to the state to arrest them. They'd be prosecuted in a federal trial court, by lawyers who work for the Department of Justice (DOJ) under the President in the federal executive branch. If the jury in the federal court convicted the KKK members, then they would be sent to federal prison.

E. Individual Rights

In addition to setting out the structure of the government, a constitution (federal or state) also prohibits the government from infringing individual rights in certain ways. For example, the federal Constitution dictates that "Congress shall make no law ... abridging the freedom of speech." Imagine that Congress passes a law saying that anyone who criticizes the government will be guilty of a crime and imprisoned accordingly. A guy named Joe Smith criticizes the government and is arrested by the FBI and prosecuted by the DOJ in federal trial court. The trial judge has the power to acquit Joe Smith on the ground that the law violates the federal Constitution, which trumps all other laws.

---

[5] The U.S. Constitution grants the U.S. Congress the power only to write laws that fit within certain categories listed in the Constitution. But one of those categories—regulation of interstate commerce—has been interpreted so broadly as to include nearly any law Congress could write.

The same thing could happen in a state court, if a state legislature passed a law that violated the state constitution. In addition, most "individual rights" provisions of the federal Constitution apply to state governments as well as to the federal government, so a state judge could rule that a state law violates the federal Constitution and is therefore void. By contrast, federal laws need not comply with state constitutions.

II.　How the Courts Work

A.　The Four Kinds of Law

As we've just seen, a *constitution* (state or federal) is the highest law in the American government structure.

The second highest law is any law passed ("enacted") by a legislature—either the federal Congress or a state legislature. These laws are called *statutes*; the definition of the word "statute" is simply "a law enacted by a legislature."

The third highest law is a law created by an agency (part of the state or federal executive branch, like the Environmental Protection Agency or the Federal Communications Commission). These laws are called *regulations*, and they are often very detailed and specific. Agencies write ("promulgate") regulations to flesh out the requirements of a statute, which usually is broader and more general than a regulation.

There is a fourth and final source of law: *common law*. This is law made entirely by courts. A legislature or agency can override common law by enacting a statute or promulgating a regulation that contradicts what the courts have said (so long as the statute or regulation does not violate the constitution). But in the absence of such a statute or regulation, the common law is binding like any other law.

B.   State and Federal Courts

1.   General Jurisdiction and Limited Jurisdiction

The example about the Ku Klux Klan involved criminal law—the area of law in which the government prosecutes an individual. But most law is civil and involves one person or company suing another. Let's say I hire a moving company to transport my belongings to my new home. The U.S. Department of Transportation (DOT—a federal agency within the executive branch) has promulgated regulations that dictate how much money moving companies are allowed to charge their customers. If my movers overcharge me, then I can sue them for failing to obey the DOT regulations.

Where will I file the lawsuit? Because the movers violated federal law (a federal agency's regulations), I can sue them in federal court. Or I can instead sue them in state court. This is because state courts are courts of *general jurisdiction*: You can bring a lawsuit in state court regardless whether the suit involves state or federal law. By contrast, federal courts are courts of *limited jurisdiction*. You can bring a lawsuit in federal court only if it meets certain requirements, such as that the suit involves primarily federal law, or that the plaintiff and defendant are from different states and the suit involves a substantial amount of money.

2. The Levels of Courts: Trial, Appeals, and Supreme

If you bring a lawsuit in federal court, it begins at the trial level. The federal trial courts are called *federal district courts*, as seen in the chart earlier in this chapter. Whoever loses at trial can appeal to a *federal court of appeals*, also known as a federal circuit court. Whoever loses in the court of appeals can ask the *U.S. Supreme Court* to hear the case and to overturn the decision of the court of appeals.[6] But the Supreme Court agrees to hear only a tiny fraction of the cases that it is asked to decide.

Things work the same way at the state level. A lawsuit starts in a state trial court, and the loser can appeal to the state court of appeals. Whoever loses in the court of appeals can ask the state's highest court (often, but not always, called the state supreme court) to hear the case.

If a case brought in state court involves *federal law* (i.e., the U.S. Constitution, or a statute enacted by the U.S. Congress, or a regulation promulgated

---

[6] Asking the Supreme Court to hear a case is called "petitioning for a writ of certiorari," or "filing a cert. petition."

by a federal agency), and that case is appealed all the way up to the state's highest court, then whoever loses in that highest court can ask the U.S. Supreme Court to hear the case and overturn the top state court. This is because the U.S. Supreme Court is the highest authority on the meaning of federal law. (Note that such an appeal would go straight to the U.S. Supreme Court, bypassing the federal district courts and the federal courts of appeals.)

However, if a case is brought in state court under *state law* (i.e., under the state constitution, or a statute passed by the state legislature, or a regulation promulgated by a state agency), then the highest state court is the final authority for that case. The state court's decision cannot be reviewed or overturned by the U.S. Supreme Court, because no federal court (not even the U.S. Supreme Court) can overrule a state court as to the meaning of state law.

3. Precedent

a) State Courts

Whenever a court makes a decision, that decision must be followed by the courts below it. Let's say that the California legislature passes a statute restricting hate speech, and a state prosecutor seeks to convict Mary Jones for speaking hatefully after the law was passed. The case will be heard in a California trial court, where Mary Jones might argue that the statute violates the California Constitution, which states that a "law may not restrain or abridge liberty of speech."[7] Suppose the state trial judge rules against Jones, and she is convicted. She appeals to the state court of appeals, which also rejects her argument, and finally to the state supreme court, where she loses once again.

After Mary Jones's appeals end, the state prosecutes Jim Williams for engaging in the same hateful speech as Jones. If Williams argues in a state trial court (or eventually in a state court of appeals) that the statute is unconstitutional, he will lose. Those courts cannot ignore the decision that the state supreme court made in the Jones case.

State courts are bound only by the decisions of higher state courts *within the same state* (or by decisions of the U.S. Supreme Court regarding federal law).[8] After the Texas Supreme Court interprets federal law in a particular way, the state courts of Louisiana or Pennsylvania (or any other state besides Texas) are still free to interpret the same federal law differently. A trial court in one state is not bound even by a supreme court in another.

b) Federal Courts

The same is true at the federal level. All federal district courts and federal courts of appeals must abide by the decisions of the U.S. Supreme Court.

---

[7] Jones could also argue that the state statute violates the U.S. Constitution.

[8] However, state courts are not bound by (i.e., not required to follow) decisions of federal courts of appeals or federal district courts.

The federal district courts and the federal courts of appeals are organized geographically into thirteen "circuits." For example, the federal courts in Maine, New Hampshire, Massachusetts, and Rhode Island compose the First Circuit;[9] the federal courts in New York, Vermont, and Connecticut compose the Second Circuit; the federal courts in Pennsylvania, New Jersey, and Delaware compose the Third Circuit;[10] and so on. (For a good map of the circuits, go to <http://www.uscourts.gov/ courtlinks/>.) The District of Columbia has its own Circuit (the D.C. Circuit), because so many cases involve the federal government. There is also one specialized circuit court, the Federal Circuit, which handles federal cases from all over the country that involve certain designated subject areas (including patents, trademarks, veterans' benefits, international trade, and government contracts). Thus, the thirteen circuits are made up of the D.C. Circuit, the Federal Circuit, and the First through Eleventh Circuits.

Federal district courts are bound to follow decisions of federal courts of appeals *in their own circuit*. This means that when the Second Circuit interprets federal law, all district courts in New York, Vermont, and Connecticut must abide by that interpretation; but district courts in any other state need not follow it.

When a federal court decides an issue of state law, it is bound by the decisions of the highest court

[9] Puerto Rico is also in the First Circuit.

[10] The Virgin Islands are also in the Third Circuit.

of that state but not by the decisions of that state's courts of appeals or trial courts.

c) *Persuasive Authority*

Although a court is not bound by the decisions of lower courts or by decisions of any court outside its jurisdiction (e.g., its state, or its federal circuit), it will often choose to follow such decisions anyway, because it finds them persuasive. If nine federal circuits have considered a question and all ruled the same way, the tenth circuit to confront it will typically be hesitant to reach the opposite conclusion, even though it is free to do so. When considering whether to follow non-binding decisions, a court will typically evaluate the strength of the reasoning offered by those decisions, the level of the courts that rendered the decisions (a federal court of appeals will usually be taken far more seriously than a state trial court, for example), and the extent to which there is agreement among those courts.

Persuasive authority is not limited to court decisions. A court may consider scholarly books or articles, although such materials will rarely be accorded as much weight as judicial decisions. When there is a leading treatise in a field, however, that treatise might well be taken very seriously. This is all the more true if the subject matter of the case is in a specialized or technical area of the law with which the court is not particularly familiar.

III. Conclusion

You've now taken the first step toward being able to write a legal memo—learning the basics of American law. This step enables you to make sense of the cases and statutes you'll read during your research, and to analyze them effectively in your writing. Of course, effective writing must be clear as well as informed. We therefore turn our attention to clarity in the next chapter.

Chapter 2

HOW TO WRITE CLEAR SENTENCES

When human beings first developed a language and started talking, they did so presumably to enable one person to share her thoughts with another. Today, most speaking and writing have that same goal: The speaker aims to pass a thought from her mind into the mind of her listener or reader.

The process is fraught with difficulties. The listener or reader could easily misunderstand the thought, in whole or in part. The longer and more complicated the message is, the less likely it will be understood.

When you write a legal memo, your goal is to overcome these dangers and communicate the information you've learned in a way that makes it easy to understand and unlikely to be misinterpreted. Everyone agrees that this is the goal, but not everyone knows that it can be achieved by following only a couple of simple principles.

As you read the principles, you might notice that I myself depart from them in many sentences of this book.[11] Some of my departures are intentional, whereas others surely manifest my own limita-

---

[11] In particular, I use many abstract subjects, and I often start sentences with introductory matter rather than my subject.

tions. But as often as I depart, I do so far less than most writers. And until you've absorbed the principles and gained some experience using them, it's safer to follow them too closely than to follow them not closely enough.

If you've been told that you're a good writer, you might be hesitant to change your approach. But fear not. Good writers will actually find it easier to make the suggested adjustments and will benefit just as much from them as will bad writers. As I mentioned in the Introduction, using these principles can transform a good writer into a great one, or a bad writer into a good one. Here are the principles.

I. Subject/Verb Pairs

Do you remember what sentences looked like when you were in grade school? They probably looked something like this: "Jack woke up and climbed out of bed. He walked to the kitchen and poured himself a glass of orange juice. He drank the juice, then he put on his clothes to go to school." Is there any doubt that the reader will understand what the writer is trying to convey in sentences like that? No, because those are great sentences.

Sadly, we forget how to write like that as we get older. But it doesn't have to be that way, because the same features that make those sentences easy to understand can be applied to any thoughts you want to convey, no matter how complicated.

If I had to boil it down to one point, it would be this: **Use subject/verb pairs, especially in the first words of each sentence**. It's easy to read the sentences about Jack because they each start with an easy subject ("Jack" or "he") followed immediately by an easy verb ("woke up," "walked," and "drank"). Putting information into subject/verb pairs, where both the subject and verb are easy to understand, is the most important thing you can do.

Let's break down this idea into principles that are even simpler and easier to put to use.

A.   The First Words of a Sentence

Whenever you write anything—a legal memo, to take just one example—you can make it ten times easier to understand by doing one thing:

MAKE SURE THAT THE FIRST WORD OF EACH SENTENCE IS A SHORT, CONCRETE SUBJECT, FOLLOWED IMMEDIATELY BY A VERB.

A subject is short if it's one word (like "Jack") or one word plus an article (like "the tree"). A subject is concrete if you can see it. You can see "Jack" or "the tree," but you can't see abstract concepts like "the issue" or "the question."

1.   Three Examples

Here are some examples of how much easier a sentence can be to read if it starts with a short, concrete subject.

Example #1

BAD: The admissibility of the evidence was determined by a three-pronged test.

GOOD: The court used a three-part test to determine whether the evidence was admissible.

I hope you'll agree with me that the second sentence ("The court used....") is easier to read than the first sentence. We find it much more manageable to digest information when it starts with a subject/verb pair—a short, concrete subject followed immediately by a verb. In the first sentence, the subject ("the admissibility of the evidence") is long (five words) and abstract (you can't see admissibility, because it's a concept rather than a physical thing). In the second sentence, the first three words provide the subject and the verb.

Some of you might now be thinking that you've encountered this lesson before, in the form of the famous advice to "avoid the passive voice." But that advice is woefully incomplete, and it misses the main point of what makes sentences clear. It's true that in Example #1, the bad sentence is passive (it uses the verb "to be," in this case via the word "was") and the good one is active. But consider the following example.

Example #2

BAD: The question whether the chicken or egg came first baffles us.

GOOD: We are baffled by the question whether the chicken or egg came first.

The first sentence is active ("baffles") whereas the second is passive ("are baffled"), but the second is much easier to read because it begins with a short, concrete subject ("we") followed immediately by a verb ("are baffled"). The active voice is often better than the passive voice, but only because it usually causes the writer to start a sentence with a subject/verb pair.

Example #3

BAD: The issue whether to question Jill weighed on the officers' minds.

GOOD: The officers thought about whether to question Jill.

Here, both sentences are in the active voice, but the second one is much better. Look how long it takes to get to the verb in the first sentence: The verb ("weighed") is the *seventh* word of the sentence. No wonder it's hard to read. You need to get to the verb much earlier, as the good sentence does ("thought" is the third word). The bad sentence fails because the subject ("the issue whether to question Jill") is far too long. And to make matters even worse, it's also abstract: If you think you can see an issue, then tell me where it is. Abstractions require the reader to exert some mental energy to understand them, and that detracts from the energy the reader can spend on understanding everything else.

I recognize that the two sentences in Example #3 do not have identical meanings. The bad sentence might aim to convey not just that the officers thought about the issue, but that it worried or troubled them. If so, this could still be conveyed via a subject/verb pair at the start of the sentence, e.g., "The officers worried about whether to question Jill."

You might think that certain nuances of meaning cannot be captured as well by an early subject/verb pair as they can by a sentence like the bad one in Example #3. For the sake of argument, let's say you're right. Maybe it follows that in certain types of writing (like fiction), my advice needs to be qualified. But I've never seen a nuance of legal reasoning that couldn't be expressed via clear, subject/verb writing. Legal writing isn't about those sorts of nuances; it's about presenting information and analysis in as clear and organized a way as possible. In a legal memo, clarity is king.

2. The Four Essentials

As I've been saying, the core rule of clear writing is to start sentences with a short, concrete subject followed immediately by a verb. That rule has four parts: (1) use a short subject, (2) use a concrete subject, (3) put the subject at the start of the sentence, and (4) follow the subject immediately with a verb.

The first three examples illustrated these points, but to leave nothing to chance, let's spend a brief moment revisiting each of them separately.

a) Use a Short Subject

As noted above, the reader needs to *get to the verb quickly*. This isn't possible if the subject is long. Take a look at the following two versions of the same sentence:

BAD: One senior partner, four junior partners, eight associates, and five paralegals took me to dinner.

GOOD: I was taken to dinner by one senior partner, four junior partners, eight associates, and five paralegals.

As in Example #2 above, here the passive voice drastically improves the sentence by enabling it to start with a subject/verb pair. We get to the verb in the second and third words, rather than in the twelfth.

This also illustrates a larger principle that can be applied throughout your writing: Leave *complicated* or *multi-word* information—stuff that's hard for the reader—until the end of the sentence. When a sentence starts with such information, it places a huge burden on the reader.

b) Use a Concrete Subject

As explained above, a subject is concrete if you can see it. It's easier for us to understand what we read if we can visualize it, so abstractions place a strain on a reader.

Bad subjects: "the standard," "the issue," "the question," "the reason," "the dispute," "Bill's insistence"

Good subjects: "the court," "the officers," "Bill," "Smith"

Let me say one thing about "the court," which is a bit of a special case. "The court" qualifies as a concrete subject even though it's really on the borderline. If we say, "The court used a three-part test," can we really visualize the court using that test? Surely the court*house* isn't using any test; it's just standing there, inanimate. Does this mean that the court is an abstraction?

Not really; it's a euphemism. In American legal writing, we say "court" when we mean "judge" or "judges." Judges typically refer to themselves or to other judges as "the court." Maybe this is due to our desire to see judicial decisions as more than just exercises of power by individuals—to see them instead as products of a legitimate legal structure adopted with the consent of the people. In any event, we *can* visualize a judge sitting at her computer and writing an opinion that uses a three-part test. And in law, everyone knows that's what you mean when you say "the court." As a result, "the court" is an acceptable and very useful subject when you write a legal memo.

c) *The Subject Should Be the First Word of the Sentence*

People love to start sentences with introductory phrases like "On June 15," or with throat-clearing wastes of time like "It is fair to assume that," or with brief asides followed by a comma. This can burden your readers and make their job more difficult.

Instead, you should start your sentences with the subject.

BAD: At 8:00 a.m. on October 20, Joe woke up and pulled himself out of bed.

GOOD: Joe woke up and pulled himself out of bed at 8:00 a.m. on October 20.

This rule dovetails with the rule about keeping the subject short, in that both rules push the verb toward the beginning of the sentence. The verb arrives at word two of the good sentence and at word eight of the bad one. Moreover, it's easier to digest the word "Joe" than the words "At 8:00 a.m. on October 20."

The rule accommodates minor exceptions like these, of course: "When Joe woke up, he saw a bear outside the tent," or "If we go to the movies, then we will be late for dinner." In these sentences, the subject is the second word rather than the first. There's nothing wrong with that, but don't get carried away. Don't lose sight of the rule by focusing on the exceptions.

d) Put No Words Between the Subject and the Verb

There are three ways for a writer to err by pushing her verb too far back in a sentence: (1) using a long, multi-word subject; (2) putting words before the subject; and (3) putting words between the subject and the verb. All are big mistakes, but we've discussed only the first two so far.

Phrases, *offset by commas*, force readers to hold their breath while waiting for the verb. This requires mental energy that would be better spent pondering the substance of the writer's points. It's much easier for the reader if the subject and verb appear in a *pair*, rather than as two entities divided by other words.

BAD: Maggie, who knows professional wrestling is fake, still likes to watch it.

GOOD: Maggie likes to watch professional wrestling even though she knows it is fake.

B. After the Beginning of the Sentence

You will write well if the first words of your sentences are subject/verb pairs. What happens after those crucial first words matters less, but it still matters. And you can fix the middle and end of a sentence the same way you fixed the beginning: by conveying the information with subject/verb pairs (short, concrete subjects followed immediately by verbs).

BAD: Prior to *Miranda*, the admissibility of custodial confessions was determined by an inquiry into whether the confession was voluntary, and voluntariness was determined by considering the totality of the circumstances.

GOOD: Before *Miranda*, courts would admit a custodial confession into evidence if they deemed that the suspect confessed voluntarily, in light of all the circumstances.

The bad sentence makes the reader's eyes glaze and might well require more than one reading to understand its point. Although the good sentence starts not with a subject but with an introductory phrase, that phrase is very short, and the rest of the sentence uses subject/verb pairs relentlessly: "courts would admit," "they deemed," "the suspect confessed."

You can always convert information into subject/verb pairs, both at the beginning of sentences and later on. Just create subjects by asking yourself *who is doing* the act you're describing. In the bad sentence above, the subjects are unnamed, but they exist: *Courts* are determining the admissibility and are inquiring into voluntariness, and *the suspect* has confessed. Once you realize what the hidden subjects are, it's easy to restate the information using subject/verb pairs, as in the good sentence.

II. Start Each Sentence with Familiar Information

As I've emphasized above, how you start your sentences will determine whether your writing is easy to read. There are two elements of starting a sentence well: (1) using a subject/verb pair (i.e., making sure that the sentence's first word is a short, concrete subject, and following that subject immediately with a verb); and (2) using a subject that the reader has already seen in recent sentences.

New information can be just as hard to digest as long subjects, abstract subjects, words that precede the subject, and words that come between the subject and the verb.

A. Two Examples

Example #1

BAD SECOND SENTENCE: Supreme Court clerks spend much of their time reading petitions for certiorari. Someone who has lost her case in a lower court may request that the Supreme Court review and overturn the decision, by filing such a petition.

GOOD SECOND SENTENCE: Supreme Court clerks spend much of their time reading petitions for certiorari. A petition for certiorari is a request that the Supreme Court review and overturn the decision of a lower court.

Example #2

BAD SECOND SENTENCE: That political strategist is notorious for push polling. When interviewers call potential voters, tell them false or misleading information about the opposing candidate, and then poll the voters on how this information will affect their votes, they are engaging in push polling.

GOOD SECOND SENTENCE: That political strategist is notorious for push polling. Push polling occurs when interviewers call potential voters, tell them false or misleading information about the opposing candidate, and then poll the voters on how this information will affect their votes.

Notice that in each example, the good second sentence uses the passive voice. My point is not that the passive voice is good, or that it's better than the active voice. Usually, the active voice is preferable. But the passive voice isn't always bad; it can be good when it enables you to start your sentence with a subject/verb pair and familiar information.

In Example #2, the bad second sentence starts with a perfect subject/verb pair (after a tiny detour for the word "when"): "Interviewers" is a short, concrete subject, and it's followed immediately by the verb "call." The problem isn't the failure to start with a subject/verb pair; it's the failure to start with a subject that the reader has seen recently. The reader hasn't been introduced yet to "interviewers" but has been introduced to "push polling," which is why the good second sentence makes the reader's task so much easier.

Of course you'll often need to introduce new information; the point is just not to introduce it at the start of a sentence. After the good second sentence in Example #2, "interviewers" could be the first word of the next sentence, because by then it's already been introduced in the middle of an earlier sentence.

B. Stick with the Same Subject

The easiest way to start each sentence with familiar information is to use the same subject again and again. This isn't an obvious point, and it's very important. Consider this example:

BAD PARAGRAPH: Jane teaches third-grade students. Each school day demands hours of preparing for class by creating a lesson, several worksheets, and model answers. Parents eager to discuss their children's progress meet with Jane frequently. Faculty meetings are held regularly, and they require her participation. Melanie, who runs the school, meets with Jane often to discuss developments in the class. Bill and Sarah are Jane's children, who also require her attention.

GOOD PARAGRAPH: Jane teaches third-grade students. She spends hours preparing for every school day by creating a lesson, several worksheets, and model answers. She also takes time to meet with parents who are eager to discuss their children's progress. She participates in faculty meetings and regularly reports to Melanie, who runs the school, on developments in the class. She somehow finds time to keep track of her own children, Bill and Sarah, too.

The good paragraph starts every sentence with the same subject ("Jane," which quickly morphs into "she"), whereas the bad paragraph introduces a new subject for each sentence. This difference makes the good paragraph much more coherent and easier to read than the bad one.

Notice that using the same subject in every sentence doesn't make the good paragraph monotonous or odd-sounding. In this context, *variety is bad*. What will make your writing interesting and engaging is its content, not different words at the start of sentences. When a sentence begins, you don't want the reader to have to spend any time wondering who or what this new subject is.

III.   Use Short, Simple Words

Just as taxicab drivers know many routes to the same destination, writers know many ways to say the same thing. In particular, there's usually a fancy way and a simple way, and *the simple way is better*.

When a reader sees a long or complicated word, there are two problems. First, he might not know what it means. In that case he'll either have to look it up in a dictionary (unlikely) or try to understand it from its context. This can lead to big misunderstandings—precisely what you want to avoid. Second, the reader might know what the fancy word means, but only after pausing to think about it. As I've been stressing throughout this chapter, your goal is to let the reader conserve all of his energy for thinking about the substance of your ideas,

33

rather than making him strain to figure out what those ideas are in the first place.

Another reason for you not to use complicated words is that *you* might not know what they mean. If you listen closely, you'll observe this phenomenon everywhere. It's deceptively difficult to use words correctly, and people misuse them all the time when they stray from very simple, familiar ones. Obviously, this is a killer in legal writing. The best way to be sure you mean what you say is to use only short, easy words in your writing.

Once you learn what a word means, it's always hard to remember that many other people don't know it. But it's critical to keep that in mind, and to accept that you're writing for someone else rather than for yourself. It's necessary but not sufficient for you to know what you mean; you also have to be sure the reader will know. So when you learn that "inter alia" means "among other things," or that "ipso facto" means "by that fact itself," this doesn't give you a license to use those terms in your writing—*ever*. Why would you, when you could use the simple English equivalents instead, and the reader is sure to understand them? Using the Latin is like writing "utilize" instead of "use": It gains you nothing and creates the danger of a misunderstanding.

You might think that your boss or your clients will be impressed by fancy words and won't view you as smart or knowledgeable or "lawyerly" if you write simply. You're just going to have to trust me when I tell you that nothing could be further from

34

the truth. Bosses and clients care about the bottom line. When they've asked you to answer a legal question, they want to know what the answer is and why. If you explain it to them clearly, they'll appreciate your work far more than that of a lawyer who makes the answer (and the reasoning) hard for them to grasp. Clients are desperate for clear writing rather than legal jargon, and the few lawyers who give them what they want tend to meet with great approval and success.

IV. Summary

Here are the three most important things to remember:

A. Start each sentence with a short, concrete subject followed immediately by a verb, and also put information later in the sentence into subject/verb pairs.

B. Start each sentence with familiar information, typically by repeating the same subject again and again.

C. Always use simple words.

V. A Note on Grammar

Some people care a lot about rules of grammar and usage—things like "Never end a sentence with a preposition," "Never split an infinitive," "Never begin a sentence with a conjunction (like 'because' or 'and') or with an adverb (like 'however' or 'nevertheless')," and on and on.

I can understand those people because I used to be one of them. But then I read a great book by Joseph Williams called *Style: Toward Clarity and Grace*. That book taught me many of the points I've made in this chapter, and it also gave me a new outlook on grammar. Williams notes that grammar rules didn't come down from the heavens, or even from some commission of writers and teachers charged with creating a helpful system. The rules were invented by people who stood to gain by publishing grammar textbooks.

In my view, the huge popularity of grammar rules has been fueled not just by the profit motive of such authors, but also by a compulsive streak that many of us have—a need for rules and order for the rules' own sake. But if we give in to that compulsive streak, we sacrifice a lot. The most obvious reason is that in many cases, a thought can be expressed most clearly by violating a traditional grammar rule. When we have a choice between clarity and rules, clarity must win: A rule that makes writing worse rather than better serves no purpose whatsoever. There's also another problem with grammar rules: They're an enormous waste of time. Why should writers and readers spend huge amounts of time learning and following these rules, when they could be spending the time improving the clarity or substance of their writing? Unless the rules help your writing achieve its goal—which, in the case of a legal memo and most other non-fiction, is clarity—there is nothing to be gained by learning or following them.

As Williams points out, if good writers often violate a rule, then it isn't a rule. The rules I mentioned in the first paragraph of this section are all violated frequently by good writers, so they're meaningless. Neither someone who writes a grammar book, nor someone who reads one and believes it, has the authority to decree it ''wrong'' to violate those rules.

Sometimes the clearest way to express a point is to follow the rules, and sometimes the clearest way is to violate them. So my advice is to ignore the rules and focus directly on clarity.

Chapter 3

ORGANIZING A LEGAL MEMO

Now we get to the nuts and bolts of how you create the document that your boss wants. Once you know the answer to her question—from the legal research you've done (or perhaps if you're a law student, from the materials your legal writing instructor has given you)—you need to convey what it is and why.

The simplest way to do this might be to write the sort of essay you wrote in high school and college: a series of paragraphs that explain the question, summarize the legal rules governing the issue (i.e., the relevant constitutional provisions, statutes, regulations, and/or cases),[12] apply those rules to the facts of your case, and give your conclusion about the likely outcome. As it turns out, you'll write that sort of essay *within* the legal memo (it's called the Discussion Section), but it's not the whole memo.[13]

[12] Most legal questions don't require you to discuss all four of these types of law. Although regulations and constitutional provisions are sometimes relevant, you'll probably deal mostly with statutes and (especially) with cases.

[13] Sometimes it can be the whole memo. If you've been asked a very small, simple question, it might be unnecessary to write the standard five-section memo; an essay will suffice. Just write the essay in the way you'd write a Discussion Section, as described in this chapter.

Why not? These memos are designed to give the reader information in a way that makes it very accessible—very easy to find what's most important or what the reader is interested in at a particular moment. A memo achieves that goal by supplying, in addition to the main essay, four shorter sections that summarize various key parts of the essay. The first section explains what the question is; the second gives the answer; the third sets forth the facts of your client's case; and the fourth quotes the relevant statutes (and constitutional provisions, if any).

In a way, a legal memo takes five sections to accomplish what could be done in one. But although this redundancy makes a memo somewhat inelegant, it also makes it user-friendly. And the goal, of course, is to make the reader's job easy.

I. The Structure of a Legal Memo

A. The Headings

Before the five sections begin, you need to put some headings at the top of the first page. Here's what those headings look like:

MEMORANDUM

TO: [the name of whomever you're giving the memo to]
FROM: [your name]
DATE: [the date on which you're handing in the memo]

RE: [a few words that summarize the sub-
            ject of the memo]

Let's say you work at a law firm, and a partner
tells you that the firm has a new client named
Vivian Hamilton. Hamilton sold an air conditioner
to a man named Jim Ford, who was dissatisfied and
refused to pay for it even though he had signed a
contract. So Hamilton came to your law firm to find
out whether she'd win if she sued Ford, and your
boss asked you to learn the answer and explain it in
a memo. For the sake of this example, we'll say that
your name is Michael Wilson and that your boss's
name is Maria Davis. The memo is due on February
9, 2007, and you're going to submit it on that day.
Here's how the headings would look:

MEMORANDUM

TO:	Maria Davis
FROM:	Michael Wilson
DATE:	February 9, 2007
RE:	Vivian Hamilton litigation

Some firms will have templates for their memos, and the headings might be formatted in slightly
different ways from the example above. That's fine.
The important thing is just to convey who's writing
the memo, who's receiving it, when it was submit-
ted, and what it's about. I will, however, make one
tiny stylistic point before moving on. I think it looks
better when the names, date, and subject are
aligned as you see them above. It would look worse
like this:

40

TO: Maria Davis

FROM: Michael Wilson

DATE: February 9, 2007

RE: Vivian Hamilton litigation

You can use the Tab key on your computer (rather than the space bar) after the colons to line up neatly the names, date, and subject.

B. The Five Sections

The five sections of a memo are as follows:

1. Introduction

2. Brief Answer

3. Facts

4. Applicable Statutes

5. Discussion

I recommend centering and boldfacing each one. So, before you fill in all the text of your memo, its skeleton looks like this:

MEMORANDUM

TO:	Maria Davis
FROM:	Michael Wilson
DATE:	February 9, 2007
RE:	Vivian Hamilton litigation

I. Introduction

II. Brief Answer

III. Facts

IV. Applicable Statutes

V. Discussion

Now all you need to do is write each section. We'll start at the beginning.

1. Section 1: The Introduction

Some people call their first section a "Question Presented" rather than an "Introduction," and they use the section as only a single question or series of questions. For example, they might write:

I. Question Presented

Did Jim Ford breach his contract with Vivian Hamilton, our client, when he refused to pay for her air conditioner?

* * *

The problem with the above approach is that it conveys too little information. The reader gets almost nothing out of the question. So people try to solve the problem by beefing up the question:

I. Question Presented

Did Jim Ford breach his contract with Vivian Hamilton, our client, when he refused to pay for the air conditioner she installed in his art gallery because he (a) found the vents unattractive, (b) objected that the thermostat offered only even-numbered temperature degrees, and (c) believed that the temperature could not be changed fast enough?

* * *

This is better, but it still leaves out all the legal issues that will be relevant. And including those issues would create its own problems:

I. Question Presented

Is an air conditioner in an art gallery more functional or aesthetic, and does a contract authorize a buyer to reject a product on unreasonable grounds if the contract states that the product must be "approved by" the buyer?

* * *

This latest version gives the main legal issues, but it says nothing about Hamilton or Ford.

To include everything relevant, people either write a very long Question Presented, or they write several questions. But even with several questions, a writer is limited by having to convey everything in the form of questions. That form often makes it difficult to introduce the reader to the parties and basic facts involved. For this reason, I advise you not to use a Question Presented and instead to use an Introduction that looks like this:

I. Introduction

This memorandum analyzes whether Jim Ford breached his contract with Vivian Hamilton, our client. Ford bought an air conditioning unit for his art gallery from Hamilton but refused to pay because he claimed he was not satisfied with Hamilton's work.

The main issue is whether Ford has the right to be unreasonable in rejecting the air conditioner. Ordinarily, a buyer must be reasonable if what he buys is primarily functional, whereas he is allowed to reject something unreasonably if it is primarily aesthetic. However, a buyer may reject even a functional product unreasonably if the contract states clearly enough that he has that right.

If the air conditioner is functional and the contract does not expressly give Ford the right to act unreasonably, then the court will assess whether a reasonable person in Ford's situation would have rejected Hamilton's work.

On the other hand, if Ford was not required to be reasonable, then the court will consider whether he was honestly dissatisfied with Hamilton's work. Even if Ford were allowed to reject the work unreasonably, he would still not be permitted to withhold payment if he feigned dissatisfaction in order to escape from his obligations under the contract.

* * *

This format frees you from the constraints of a Question Presented, allowing you to mix in whatever facts and legal issues you think are most relevant. Notice that the Introduction starts at a general level and then becomes more specific. It names the parties immediately, explaining who they are and which one is your client. Most important, it *assumes no knowledge*. It's always better to risk telling a reader what she already knows than to risk leaving out something she doesn't.

The main point of the Introduction is to break down the question you've been given (in this case, "Who will win?") into whatever sub-issues there are, and to give a very brief preview of those sub-issues. As I discussed in the chapter on writing clear sentences, you should spell everything out in simple words without any legal jargon.

If we put the headings together with the Introduction, then the first page of the memo looks like this:

MEMORANDUM

TO:	Maria Davis
FROM:	Michael Wilson
DATE:	February 9, 2007
RE:	Vivian Hamilton litigation

I. Introduction

This memorandum analyzes whether Jim Ford breached his contract with Vivian Hamilton, our client. Ford bought an air conditioning unit for his art gallery from Hamilton but refused to pay because he claimed he was not satisfied with Hamilton's work.

The main issue is whether Ford has the right to be unreasonable in rejecting the air conditioner. Ordinarily, a buyer must be reasonable if what he buys is primarily functional, whereas he is allowed to reject something unreasonably if it is primarily aesthetic. However, a buyer may reject even a functional product unreasonably if the contract states clearly enough that he has that right.

If the air conditioner is functional and the contract does not expressly give Ford the right to act unreasonably, then the court will assess whether a reasonable person in Ford's situation would have rejected Hamilton's work.

On the other hand, if Ford was not required to be reasonable, then the court will consider whether he was honestly dissatisfied with Hamilton's work. Even if Ford were allowed to reject the work unreasonably, he would still not be permitted to withhold payment if he feigned dissatisfaction in order to escape from his obligations under the contract.

* * *

2. Section 2: The Brief Answer

More than anything else, your boss wants to know the final answer to the question she gave you. So it's essential to have a section early in the memo revealing that answer. Here's a sample:

II. Brief Answer

Ford probably breached the contract by withholding payment.

The court will likely rule that Ford needed to be reasonable. First, an air conditioner (even in an art gallery) is primarily functional rather than aesthetic. Second, the contract does not state with sufficient clarity that Ford has the right to reject Hamilton's work even if a reasonable person would have accepted it.

Ford is unreasonable in at least two of his three objections to Hamilton's work (that he found the vents unattractive, and that the thermostat offered only even-numbered degrees of temperature). We can decide whether his third objection (that the air conditioner does not change the temperature of the gallery fast enough) is reasonable only by learning how quickly the temperature changes. If the temperature changes at a rate that is normal for a room of that size—and we have no reason yet to believe otherwise—then all of Ford's complaints are unreasonable and he has breached the contract.

In the unlikely event the court were to decide that Ford need not be reasonable, Ford would not have breached the contract. There is no evidence that Ford lied when he said he was dissatisfied, and such deceit is very difficult to prove without direct evidence like an admission.

* * *

It's important for the Introduction and Brief Answer to link together tightly. The Brief Answer should address the same issues the Introduction sets forth, typically in the same order, and explain how those issues will be resolved. As always, the writing should be simple and clear.

Note that in the Brief Answer, *the first sentence answers the overall question you were asked.* You get into the sub-issues only after revealing the bottom line.

3. Section 3: The Facts

After you tell the reader the questions and answers (i.e., the issues and likely results), you need to explain what happened in your case. In the Discussion Section, you'll flesh out the legal rules and apply them to those facts, but the reader also needs a place where all the facts are laid out together in an orderly, easy-to-understand way.

Often, the best way to lay out those facts is to tell the story in chronological order. But there are exceptions. If a case involves multiple issues, each of which is very complicated and involves facts that overlap chronologically with those of the other issues, then you might want to organize the Facts Section by issue (with a subheading for each issue) rather than purely by date. Even then, I'd probably go chronologically within each issue.

In the Facts Section, your goal is to be comprehensive without being unfocused. *The Facts Section must include every fact from your case that will be mentioned in the Discussion Section*, and the ideal Facts Section would mention only those facts and no others. You don't want to waste the reader's time with a long recounting of tangential, unnecessary facts. But you do want to make sure that everything relevant is in there. Some writers try to achieve this balance by writing the Facts Section after they've written the Discussion Section, because only then can they be sure which facts are relevant and which aren't.

In a long memo, the first paragraph of the Facts Section should give a very brief background about how the lawsuit arose. It should explain who is suing (or prosecuting) whom, and for what. As in the Introduction, you should always say at the outset which party your firm or organization is representing, if applicable. Here's an example of a Facts Section with such an opening paragraph:

III. Facts

Max Graham, our client, was stopped and questioned by two law enforcement officers at O'Hare Airport on June 15, 2006. The officers ultimately searched his luggage and found cocaine. Graham was convicted of drug possession in federal district court in Chicago. He is now considering appealing the conviction on the ground that the questioning constituted an unreasonable seizure under the Fourth Amendment to the U.S. Constitution.

Graham arrived at O'Hare on a flight from Los Angeles and was walking through the terminal when the two officers approached him. They wore jackets marked "Police" and "DEA" but were otherwise dressed in plain clothes. They explained that they wanted to talk to Graham about a drug-trafficking investigation, and Graham consented. The officers then led him into a small room off the crowded main hallway of the terminal, and they left the door open.

Graham sat across a table from the officers, who removed their jackets and thereby made visible their holstered guns. The officers asked a few questions about Graham's stay in Los Angeles, then noted that they suspected him of drug trafficking. They then asked whether Graham would answer a few more questions, and Graham simply stared straight ahead in response. The officers continued to question Graham, who continued to give answers.

Finally, the officers requested permission to search Graham's luggage. Graham consented upon being told that if he refused, the officers could temporarily detain the luggage while a narcotics-detecting dog sniffed it. The officers found cocaine in the luggage.

* * *

In a short memo, an introductory paragraph might be unnecessary in the Facts Section. You can just dive right in:

III.   Facts

Jim Ford hired Vivian Hamilton, our client, to install an air conditioning system in Ford's art gallery in Elkhart, Indiana. Ford's lawyer drafted the contract, which stated:

(1) Hamilton Heating and Cooling agrees to install a functional central air-conditioning system in the Ford Gallery.

(2) Because the system will cool an exhibition space, no condenser units or any other parts may jut out into the gallery, or obstruct or otherwise interfere with the viewing of the art.

(3) A digital thermostat will be located in Ford's office, so that he may easily adjust the temperature to meet the particular needs of the gallery's visitors.

(4) If the work is completed by June 1, 2006, and approved by Ford, then Ford will pay Hamilton $15,000 by June 15, 2006.

Hamilton completed the work on May 31, 2006. On June 15, Hamilton received a letter from Ford stating that he refused to pay for three reasons: (1) "I think the vents are unattractive because their color, though pale like the gallery walls, has a red undertone that clashes with the green undertone in the walls"; (2) "The thermostat allows me to set the temperature only at even-numbered levels like 70°F or 72°F, which is inadequate because I sometimes want to set it at 71°F'"; and (3) "The temperature does not change quickly enough to suit my guests." The letter went on to request that Hamilton remove the air conditioning system.

Hamilton seeks to sue Ford for $15,000 in Indiana state court.

* * *

As you can see from the Hamilton/Ford example, it's essential in the Facts Section to *quote everything relevant* and avoid paraphrasing. The reader will typically flip to this section to find a definitive account of what happened, including specific points whose small details might ultimately become important. If you paraphrase, then the reader might have to look beyond the memo to other materials to find what she's looking for, and that's always bad. You want the Facts Section, and the memo generally, to provide one-stop shopping.

So, the headings plus the first three sections would look like this:

MEMORANDUM

TO:	Maria Davis
FROM:	Michael Wilson
DATE:	February 9, 2007
RE:	Vivian Hamilton litigation

I. Introduction

This memorandum analyzes whether Jim Ford breached his contract with Vivian Hamilton, our client. Ford bought an air conditioning unit for his art gallery from Hamilton but refused to pay because he claimed he was not satisfied with Hamilton's work.

The main issue is whether Ford has the right to be unreasonable in rejecting the air conditioner. Ordinarily, a buyer must be reasonable if what he buys is primarily functional, whereas he is allowed to reject something unreasonably if it is primarily aesthetic. However, a buyer may reject even a functional product unreasonably if the contract states clearly enough that he has that right.

If the air conditioner is functional and the contract does not expressly give Ford the right to act unreasonably, then the court will assess whether a reasonable person in Ford's situation would have rejected Hamilton's work.

On the other hand, if Ford was not required to be reasonable, then the court will consider whether he was honestly dissatisfied with Hamilton's work. Even if Ford were allowed to reject the work unreasonably, he would still not be permitted to withhold payment if he feigned dissatisfaction in order to escape from his obligations under the contract.

II. Brief Answer

Ford probably breached the contract by withholding payment.

The court will likely rule that Ford needed to be reasonable. First, an air conditioner (even in an art gallery) is primarily functional rather than aesthetic. Second, the contract does not state with sufficient clarity that Ford has the right to reject Hamilton's work even if a reasonable person would have accepted it.

Two of Ford's three objections to Hamilton's work (that he found the vents unattractive, and that the thermostat offered only even-numbered degrees of temperature) are clearly unreasonable. We can decide whether the third objection (that the air conditioner does not change the temperature of the gallery fast enough) is reasonable only by learning how quickly the temperature changes. If the temperature changes at a rate that is normal for a room of that size—and we have no reason yet to believe otherwise—then Ford was unreasonable and has breached the contract.

In the unlikely event that the court were to decide Ford need not be reasonable, Ford would not have breached the contract. There is no evidence that Ford lied when he said he was dissatisfied, and such deceit is very difficult to prove without direct evidence such as an admission.

III. Facts

Jim Ford hired Vivian Hamilton, our client, to install an air conditioning system in Ford's art gallery in Elkhart, Indiana. Ford's lawyer drafted the contract, which stated:

(1) Hamilton Heating and Cooling agrees to install a functional central air-conditioning system in the Ford Gallery.

(2) Because the system will cool an exhibition space, no condenser units or any other parts may jut out into the gallery, or obstruct or otherwise interfere with the viewing of the art.

(3) A digital thermostat will be located in Ford's office, so that he may easily adjust the temperature to meet the particular needs of the gallery's visitors.

(4) If the work is completed by June 1, 2006, and approved by Ford, then Ford will pay Hamilton $15,000 by June 15, 2006.

Hamilton completed the work on May 31, 2006. On June 15, Hamilton received a letter from Ford stating that he refused to pay for three reasons: (1) "I think the vents are unattractive because their color, though pale like the gallery walls, has a red undertone that clashes with the green undertone in the walls"; (2) "The thermostat allows me to set the temperature only at even-numbered levels like 70°F or 72°F, which is inadequate because I sometimes want to set it at 71°F"; and (3) "The temperature does not change quickly enough to suit my guests." The letter went on to request that Hamilton remove the air conditioning system.

Hamilton seeks to sue Ford for $15,000 in Indiana state court.

* * *

4. Section 4: The Applicable Statutes

In some memos, all of the legal rules set out in the Discussion Section come from cases (judicial opinions). In those memos, you can move directly from the Facts Section to the Discussion Section. But in most memos, the legal rules will include some provisions of constitutions (state or federal) or statutes (state or federal) or both. The wording of constitutional and statutory provisions is so important to courts that it should never be paraphrased in any section of a memo. In addition, a typical memo devotes an entire section to quoting the relevant text of such provisions so the reader always knows where to look them up.

If you're quoting a constitution as well as statutes, then label the section "Constitutional and Statutory Provisions." Otherwise, call it "Applicable Statutes."

List the citations so that the reader can look up the statutes if necessary, and quote the relevant passages. But quote *only* what is relevant. Use ellipses to cut out parts of the statute that won't appear in your Discussion Section and could distract the reader from those that will. Any words you will quote from a statute in your Discussion Section, of course, must also be quoted here.

The Hamilton/Ford hypothetical case doesn't lend itself ideally to illustrating what an Applicable Statutes Section should look like, so here's an example of such a section that would apply to a different legal question. The question is whether Article 2 of the Illinois Commercial Code applies to a transaction where a good was shipped in pieces and assembled by the buyer after the purchase.

IV. Applicable Statutes

1.   810 Ill. Comp. Stat. Ann. 5/2–102 (West 2000). Scope, Certain Security and Other Transactions Excluded From This Article

> [T]his Article applies to transactions in goods . . . .

2.   810 Ill. Comp. Stat. Ann. 5/2–105 (West 2000). Definitions: Transferability; "Goods"; "Future" Goods; "Lot"; "Commercial Unit"

(1) "Goods" means all things (including specially manufactured goods) which are movable at the time of identification to the contract for sale . . . .

(2) Goods must be both existing and identified before any interest in them can pass. Goods which are not both existing and identified are "future" goods. A purported present sale of future goods or of any interest therein operates as a contract to sell.

3. 810 Ill. Comp. Stat. Ann. 5/2–106 (West 2000). Definitions: "Contract"; "Agreement"; "Contract for Sale"; "Sale"; "Present Sale"; "Conforming" to Contract; "Termination"; "Cancellation"

A "sale" consists in the passing of title from the seller to the buyer for a price . . . .

4. 810 Ill. Comp. Stat. Ann. 5/2–501 (West 2000). Insurable Interest in Goods; Manner of Identification of Goods

In the absence of explicit agreement identification occurs

(a) when the contract is made if it is for the sale of goods already existing and identified;

> (b) if the contract is for the sale of future goods . . ., when goods are shipped, marked or otherwise designated by the seller as goods to which the contract refers;

> . . . .

> Official Comment: . . . In the ordinary case identification of particular existing goods as goods to which the contract refers is unambiguous and may occur in one of many ways. It is possible, however, for the identification to be tentative or contingent. In view of the limited effect given to identification by this Article, the general policy is to resolve all doubts in favor of identification. . . .

* * *

5. Section 5: The Discussion

The Discussion Section is the essay in which you break down the overall question into sub-issues, explain the statutes and cases that create the law governing each sub-issue, apply that law to the relevant facts of your case, and note the likely outcome. Your reader should be able to learn everything important in your memo by reading only the Discussion Section.

a) *Introductory Paragraphs*

The Discussion should start with an introductory paragraph or set of paragraphs that explains how the section will be organized. These paragraphs might look a lot like the Introduction and Brief Answer, but don't worry about redundancy: The whole point of a legal memo is to be redundant by adding four sections to the only section that's really necessary—the Discussion. Because we want to save readers the time of hunting for things in this main section, we pull out the things they're most likely to want (the issues, the answers, the facts, and the statutes) and repeat those things in their own independent sections.

b) *Sub-headings*

After the introductory paragraph or paragraphs, the Discussion needs to be divided into sub-headings (and maybe sub-sub-headings, etc.). I would use an outline form similar to the one used in this book and would underline or boldface each heading. The sub-headings create the outline and organizational structure of the Discussion, and thus each should be devoted to a sub-issue that helps compose the larger question the memo exists to answer. In other words, always *organize the Discussion Section by issue, not chronologically.*

c) *IRAC*

When you've written your sub-headings, your next task is to fill in the text within each of them. Here you'll finally be writing the sentences and paragraphs of the essay that answers your boss's question. There's a formula for writing those sentences and paragraphs within each sub-heading of the Discussion Section, and it's perhaps the most famous concept in legal writing: IRAC. "IRAC" is an acronym that stands for Issue, Rule, Application, Conclusion. What it means is as follows.

i) Issue

In general, the first sentence or group of sentences within a sub-heading should explain the *issue* addressed by that section of the Discussion. (The underlined sub-heading itself could perform that function, if you make it a full sentence. Then the first sentence below the sub-heading could bypass the issue and begin the statement of the rule. It's fine to use full sentences as sub-headings, but only if you keep the sentences very short, simple, and clear.) For example, one of the issues in the Ford/Hamilton memo will be whether an air conditioner in an art gallery is primarily functional or aesthetic.

You can state an issue either in a neutral way or in a way that reveals your conclusion. For example, you might write, "The court must decide whether an air conditioner in an art gallery is primarily functional or aesthetic"; *or*, "The court will probably rule that an air conditioner in an art gallery is primarily functional rather than aesthetic."

ii) Rule

After you state the issue, you explain the legal *rule*. As noted in Chapter 1, there are four types of legal rule: constitutions, statutes, agency regulations, and cases. Secondary sources like treatises and law review articles can also be useful but are much less important. The rule that governs your issue might well be created by a combination of authorities, e.g., a constitutional provision, two statutes, and five cases. Present the rule by discussing the authorities in order *from most to least important*:

Constitution—> statutes—> regulations—> cases—> academic literature

When you start discussing cases, you should generally put those cases in order, too, starting with the ones that will be given most weight by the court that will hear your client's case. If your client's case involves state law, then the highest authority is the supreme court of that state. Next would be the state appeals courts, and then the state trial courts. (The opinion of a federal court of appeals applying the *state law* of that state would not be binding but would be very persuasive.) If your client's case involves federal law, then the highest authority would be the U.S. Supreme Court, then (assuming you're in federal court) the federal court of appeals for your jurisdiction, then the federal district courts in that jurisdiction. (Again, opinions of other federal courts of appeals would be very persuasive but non-binding.)

Cases from outside the jurisdiction will be more persuasive the higher the court is. Very old decisions tend to matter less, but they're still binding if they're in your case's jurisdiction and have never been overturned. (Of course, "binding" just means that an indistinguishable case will be decided the same way. A court will be much more willing to seize upon fine distinctions in order to reach a different result if the relevant precedent is from 1884 than if it's from two years ago.)

Unpublished cases tend to be the least meaningful, but how they are treated varies by jurisdiction. If you see at the top of an opinion that it's unpublished, and you want to include it in your memo, then you need to look up the court rules of that jurisdiction to see whether the case can be cited and how much authority it has. You also need to explain these findings in your memo.

If there are ambiguities in the legal rule that emerges from the statutes and cases you discuss, don't be afraid to acknowledge those ambiguities. If you give the reader a fair analysis of all the relevant information, along with your take on it, then the reader can ultimately decide for herself the right course of action. That's all you're being asked to do. Never feel pressure to say that a clear, certain rule exists when it doesn't.

There are two more things to note about the rule discussion, both of which are overlooked by most writers—much to their readers' chagrin. First, don't go into a long discussion of any case. Just explain the relevant reasoning and holding of the case, and at most add a *very* brief summary of the facts (maybe a couple of sentences). Second, *quote—*

don't paraphrase. With constitutions, statutes, and regulations, you're always required to quote; but I urge you to extend that rule to the relevant passages of judicial decisions as well. You help the reader much more by quoting because she then isn't limited to accepting blindly your interpretation of what the court meant. That said, *quoting must be terse and targeted*; long block quotes are hard for the reader and therefore out of place in a Discussion Section. Quote what matters and cut right to the chase, using ellipses if necessary.

iii) Application

After you've set out the legal rule, *apply* that rule to the facts of your case. This just means that you should assess how your case fits in with the other similar ones that have been decided (or with the statutes and regulations that cover it). The application is the crucial moment when you explain what the law means for your client's chances. You can't assume the reader knows everything (or anything) that's in the Facts Section. You need to restate the facts of your case that are relevant to the subsection you're writing. In the Hamilton/Ford memo, certain provisions of the contract and of Ford's letter would be quoted (*not* paraphrased) in particular parts of the Discussion Section.

iv) Conclusion

Finally, write a sentence or a small group of sentences giving your *conclusion* about the likely outcome of the issue.

d) Ending the Section and the Memo

At the end of the Discussion Section, you should have a sub-section that summarizes your analysis of which side will win each part of the question and why, and what this means for the overall question. This final sub-section will resemble the Brief Answer, but you're free to be more detailed here at the end of the memo because it's more likely the reader will now be familiar with the in-depth reasoning you've just given throughout the Discussion Section. You can make references to that reasoning without worrying as much that they'll be misunderstood. If you prefer, you can take this concluding sub-section out of the Discussion and make it instead a sixth major section of the memo.

C. Flexibility

I haven't provided a sample Discussion Section for two reasons. One is that I want to give you (and your teacher, if you're reading this book within a legal writing course) the opportunity to use the Hamilton/Ford case as an exercise in which you write your own Discussion. The other reason, perhaps more important, is that a Discussion is too complicated to reduce to one sample or even a series of samples. Giving a sample would fix in your mind the idea that the approach used in that section was "right," when really it would be right only for that memo and might be wrong for a memo on a different issue. Just as chess has virtually limitless variations and therefore can't be taught via one (or a handful of) sample games, so too with a Discussion Section.

Instead, you need to apply the principles outlined above and gain experience tweaking your rule analyses and applications to fit what's needed in a given assignment. This takes time, and there might be some growing pains, but your work will become easier and better with every memo you write.

Nothing in this chapter should become a straitjacket that hinders you from telling the reader the crucial information clearly and effectively. If you sometimes can't find a way to accomplish that goal within the parameters I've outlined, then go outside those parameters. The structure supplied in this chapter is meant to help you present your information, and in most cases I think it should work very well. But the universe of legal questions isn't reducible to any formula, so treat my suggestions as a guide that opens up possibilities rather than closing them off.

II. Summary

There's a lot to digest in this chapter, and sometimes you might want a quick reminder of the main points. For that purpose, I've supplied a Writing Checklist as the last chapter of this book. I highly recommend that you use the checklist just before you hand in a memo, to help you make sure you've remembered the things that are most important.

Chapter 4

RESEARCH

Readers want answers to their legal questions, and finding those answers might be the most important skill a lawyer can have. Before you convey the answer in a memo, you need to learn what you'll be conveying.

The answer will come from laws themselves—constitutions, statutes, regulations, and cases. But before diving into the laws, you can make your job easier by looking at sources that comment on those laws, give you background information on your topic, and point you to the right statutes and cases to read.

I. Learning the Background

There are five main sources for learning the background of your legal question: *American Law Reports*, treatises, legal encyclopedias, commercial outlines, and law review articles. Let's consider each one.

A. American Law Reports

American Law Reports (*ALR*) is a massive collection of detailed articles about legal issues. As a research tool, it tends to be hit or miss: Either you'll quickly find an article that's incredibly useful and points you to a huge number of relevant cases, or you won't find anything worth the time it takes to read. So I recommend doing a quick *ALR* search whenever you get a research assignment. If it works, then it's a goldmine; and if not, then you move on right away without having wasted much time.

You can find *ALR* either in a library or in the online legal databases of LexisNexis and Westlaw. In a library, you'd use the Index to search for articles on your topic. On Lexis, *ALR* appears under "Secondary Legal," and on Westlaw it similarly appears under "Secondary Sources." Click on the *ALR* links until you get to a box that allows you to enter search terms.

Once you see that box, you can search for an article on your topic. The simplest way is to do a "Natural Language" search—an option that appears just above the box for search terms as an alternative to "Terms and Connectors." A Natural Language search allows you to enter your topic the way you'd describe it in ordinary speech. For example, imagine you have a client who's moving from one apartment to another, and his landlord at the building he's leaving refuses to return his security deposit. Your client wants to know if he can win if he sues his landlord. In a natural Language search, you might enter these words: When can a landlord keep a security deposit?

The other option is a "Terms and Connectors" search. Here you typically select a "segment" or a "field"—i.e., a part of the article like the title or author—and enter terms that will appear in that segment. For example, you could enter "security deposit" within the Title segment to find all articles with that term in the article's title.

Once you click on the word "Search," you'll be given a list of articles that meet your search terms. You can try to skim through the titles or short descriptions to see if one looks relevant. (In a Natural Language search, your best bet will often be the first article in the list.) Click on the link to the article that seems most promising, and take a look at it. Finding the text is a bit trickier than you might expect: You often need to scroll past a seemingly endless Index and Table of Cases.

If you find what you want, then you'll be in great shape. If not, then don't dwell on *ALR*. Move on to, say, a treatise.

When you cite or quote something in your memo, it should be either a law (a constitution, statute, regulation, or case) or a scholarly treatise or law review article. Other sources like *ALR* *should not be cited*. It would be like citing the Encyclopedia Britannica—acceptable for a third-grade essay, perhaps, but not for serious writing. Sources like *ALR* help you understand the background and point you to other sources like statutes and cases, but they provide no independent support for a point.

B. Treatises

A treatise is just a book, ordinarily written by a law professor who knows a lot about the law of a particular field. For example, some leading treatises are *Couch on Insurance*; *Collier on Bankruptcy*; *Nimmer on Copyright*; *Moore's Federal Practice*; and Laurence Tribe's *American Constitutional Law*. How do you know what the leading treatise is in the area you're interested in? The best way is to ask a librarian. Failing that, you can try asking a partner or co-worker, or maybe a professor at your law school. You can also find books about your subject by simply typing the subject (e.g., "Insurance" or "Bankruptcy" or "Copyright" or "Constitutional Law" or "Contracts," etc.) into a title search in a library's online catalog. Many books with that title will appear, and you can browse them in the stacks. Still, the best approach is to find a leading treatise by asking a librarian.

Once you've found a treatise in the library,[14] look up your topic in the book's Index. There's a good chance you'll find it, and the treatise will typically give you an extremely helpful explanation of the law in the area. There are several advantages to using treatises in your research. Unlike *ALR*, commercial outlines, and legal encyclopedias, treatises *can and should be cited* in your memo, because courts care what they say. In addition, treatises

---

[14] Some treatises are also available in the online databases of Lexis and Westlaw.

usually direct you to some of the relevant statutes, regulations, and cases. They tend to be clear and reasonably easy to understand, as well as quite trustworthy as to matters of substance. One drawback is that they're rarely up-to-date.

C. Legal Encyclopedias

The two main legal encyclopedias are called *American Jurisprudence* (*Am. Jur.*) and *Corpus Juris Secundum* (*CJS*). They're in every law library. You can ask a librarian where to find them, or just type the titles into the library's online catalog.

Like a regular encyclopedia, these are organized alphabetically. So just look up your subject by its first letter.

Legal encyclopedias cover a lot and cite many cases, but they're not always easy to read and are even more out-of-date than most treatises. Like *ALR* and commercial outlines, but unlike treatises and law review articles, *Am. Jur. and CJS should not be cited* in your memo.

D. Commercial Outlines

Commercial outlines are books written to help law students study for exams. But they can also help a memo writer get a sense of the background of a legal issue if the more traditional sources fail. Two of the main examples are *Emanuel Law Out-*

lines and *Gilbert Law Summaries*, each of which has books on basic subjects like Constitutional Law, Torts, Contracts, Corporations, Tax, and many others.

Commercial outlines tend to make things easy to find, so either the Index or the Table of Contents should enable you to locate your topic.

Once you find it, you'll usually see that these outlines are easy to understand and to read quickly, and that they direct you to the most famous cases. But they're shallow, not as trustworthy as other sources, and often dated. And as unprofessional as it would be to cite *ALR* or an encyclopedia in your writing, it would be even more embarrassing (by orders of magnitude) to cite a commercial outline.

E. Law Review Articles

Law professors and students constantly publish articles and notes that can help you understand your topic and can point you to the most important cases. You find these articles on Lexis or Westlaw by looking under "Secondary Sources," then "Law Reviews and Journals" (Lexis) or "Journals and Law Reviews" (Westlaw).

Once you get to the box for search terms, follow the steps described above in the *ALR* section to find relevant articles. Then click on the articles that look useful and skim the part dealing with your search terms. You can skip to those terms by clicking the right arrow next to the word "Term" at the bottom of the screen.

Like treatises, law review articles can be cited in your memo. Don't go overboard, though; they won't be too important to either a court or your reader.

II. Finding the Relevant Law

After you've learned the background, you're ready to look for the specific laws—especially cases—that will give you the answer to your question.

One place to start is by reading cases that were referenced by the background materials. Note that those background materials are never comprehensive; no book or article covers every relevant case. To find the cases, you need to read the ones cited by the books or articles, then read the cases cited and discussed *by those cases*, and then continue using cases in this way to find other cases. The goal is to read, or at least skim, everything that looks relevant until the cases you're reading start citing (on the point at issue) only other cases you've already read. Then you know you've "completed the circle" of research.

The most common way to tackle a research task is to run a search on Lexis or Westlaw for cases containing the terms of your topic. You might first want to search in the database that contains all cases, but ultimately you'll need to search only within your case's jurisdiction (for example, you might search within a database of all state court cases in Indiana, or a database of all federal cases from the Fourth Circuit plus the U.S. Supreme Court). Skimming the cases that emerge—especially the parts of those cases that include your search terms—should let you find what's relevant. Once you find one case that's truly on-point, it'll cite and be cited by others, and you'll be on your way.

But how do you craft the search in the first place? What terms do you use? Sadly, there's no good way I know to teach this skill other than trial and error, supplemented by the basic Lexis and Westlaw training (by librarians and/or by representatives of Westlaw and Lexis) that is available at all law schools. At least I can point you to one resource that most lawyers overlook: free research phone support from Lexis and Westlaw. Whenever you have an assignment, you can call either company and ask their researchers to help you construct searches to find what you need, at no charge. Far too few people use this resource. The Lexis phone number is listed on the website if you click on "Live Support" at the top right of the screen; the number is 1–800–45–LEXIS (1–800–455–3947). For Westlaw, the number is listed directly on the front page (after you sign in), at the bottom left; it's 1–800–850–WEST (1–800–850–9378).

If you get too many search results to read them all, you can search for more specific terms *within* those results by using the "Focus" feature (Lexis) or "Locate in Result" (Westlaw).

III. Shepardizing (Lexis) and KeyCiting (Westlaw)

Lexis and Westlaw are not just useful for entering search terms. They also let you find, with one click, every case that has ever cited or discussed the case you're looking at. This tool is incredibly valuable.

Suppose you enter your search terms into a database of Indiana state courts and come up with several cases that include those terms. You skim the cases and find one that perfectly answers your question. If you immediately put that case into your memo, you run the risk that the case has been subsequently *overturned*. Lexis and Westlaw help you guard against that by means of a tool called Shepard's (Lexis) or KeyCite (Westlaw).

When you're reading a case online, there will be a symbol at the top of the screen, just to the left of the case name. Different symbols mean different things, as you can learn from the Lexis and Westlaw websites. For example, a red symbol means that at least one part of the case's holding has been overruled, and a yellow symbol means that at least one part has been questioned, distinguished, or limited in some way. Clicking on the symbol will give you a list of every case (and other source) that has cited your case. You can organize these citing references by jurisdiction, by whether they agreed or disagreed with your case, or by how extensively they discussed your case. Remember that when a case has been overruled (or limited), it might have been overruled on a point of law that's separate from—and irrelevant to—the point for which you're using it. If so, then your case is still good law for your point. You need to learn the ground on which it was overruled by clicking on and reading the case that overrules it.

Shepard's and KeyCite are also valuable as search tools. When you find a case that's on point, that case will typically cite and discuss the relevant cases that came before it. But you need Shepard's or KeyCite to point you to the relevant cases that came after it.

IV. Parting Thoughts on Research

The key to legal research is using one source to help you find others. This works especially well with cases, because they always cite other cases and are cited by other cases. Once you've found even one truly relevant case, you can probably find all the others by a combination of reading that case (to find the cases it cites, then reading those cases, then the cases they cite, until you've completed the circle) and Shepardizing it. To find the first case, do the background research and then perform searches, calling Lexis and Westlaw for help if necessary.

Try not to assume that what you're looking for doesn't exist. It's amazing how many cases are out there, and if you cast the net wide enough and are persistent, you can usually find a case that says just about anything.

Chapter 5

MORE ABOUT WRITING, CASES, AND STATUTES

Chapters 1–4 covered most of what you need to know to write a good legal memo. The only major topic remaining is legal citation, which is the subject of Chapter 6. But there are lots of miscellaneous points—some very large, some very small—that don't fit neatly into the other chapters but will be useful to you. I've broken those points into three categories (writing, cases, and statutes) and devoted this chapter to them.

I. Writing

Most of my miscellaneous writing tips are small points about form, but before we get to those, there are two crucial points about substance.

A. Substance

1. Be Objective

Most people think of lawyers as advocates—"mouthpieces" who argue on behalf of their clients. And in litigation, that's just what lawyers are. Nevertheless, writing a memo to a boss or a client is different in one enormous way from writing a piece of advocacy that will be filed in a court: The memo is *objective*.

You're *not trying to persuade* the reader of anything, but rather to *inform* her of the answer to her question. If your research shows that the client will probably lose, then that's what you need to write. And if it shows that the client will probably win, then you still can't be blind to the counter-arguments or information that cuts the other way. There will be a time for advocacy, but memo-writing isn't that time. You can't do your job as a memo writer effectively unless you approach the research and writing objectively rather than from the perspective of your client.

The need for objectivity also faces a related but different obstacle. When you've done your research and arrived at an answer, you'll need to overcome a human tendency to argue for that answer rather than to explain it in a neutral way. Whether the answer helps or hurts your client, you might feel the inclination to show that your answer is true by slanting your writing in favor of it. Don't succumb to that temptation. You need to *acknowledge the factors that cut against your conclusion*, and if an issue is close, then say it's close. Throughout the memo, be entirely evenhanded in laying out the information you've found. Don't try to fit the information into some pre-set argument; just present it in an organized fashion, noting any tensions or contradictions within the cases. Once the reader has the information, she can use it in whatever way will most help the client.

2. Give an Answer

Although you need to present the information on both sides, you also need to tell your opinion about the likely outcome of each sub-issue and the larger question. Make sure that you say who is more likely to win the case and who is more likely to win each dispute within the case, and make this clear both in the Brief Answer and in the Discussion Section.

In the sentences where you express your opinion, you can say whether the issue is close or clear; but make sure not to do so in a way that leaves your opinion vague.

BAD: The court may rule that an air conditioner in an art gallery is more functional than aesthetic.

GOOD: The court will probably rule that an air conditioner in an art gallery is more functional than aesthetic.

GOOD: The court is slightly more likely than not to rule that an air conditioner in an art gallery is more functional than aesthetic.

B. Form

With one exception, the following points about form are not enormously important. You could write a good memo even if you neglected them. But in most cases, you can make your memo a bit more professional and easier to read by taking these cues.

1. Always Use Names Rather Than Legal Labels

This suggestion is the important one. Lawyers always seem to confuse their readers by referring to people with words like "plaintiff," "defendant," "petitioner," "respondent," "appellant," and "appellee." You should *never* use any of these words. If you do, the reader will constantly be trying to remember who the plaintiff or petitioner or appellee is. Instead, *use the person's (or company's) name*, like "Vivian Hamilton," "Jim Ford," "Smith," "Jones," "AT&T," "Microsoft," etc. You can make your memos much easier to read by following this simple rule. Almost all bad writers seem to violate it.

2. Page Numbers

Include page numbers at the top right, or at the bottom center, of each page except the first one.

3. Font

I recommend Times New Roman 12–point font.

4. Margins

Use one-inch margins on all sides of the page: top, bottom, left, and right. Note that this might not be your default setting. You can check by clicking on "Format," then "Document" in Microsoft Word.

5. Spaces

Put *two spaces*—not just one—between a period and the beginning of the next sentence. If what follows the period is not the next sentence but a citation, then it's a judgment call, and either one or two spaces would be fine.

6. Underline Case Names, Even in Textual Sentences

BAD: In Ellerth, the Supreme Court laid out a framework for deciding when employers are vicariously liable for sexual harassment by supervisors.

GOOD: In Ellerth, the Supreme Court laid out a framework for deciding when employers are vicariously liable for sexual harassment by supervisors.

However, don't underline the name if you're referring to the person rather than the case.

BAD: In Smith, the court ruled that Smith had been deprived of property without due process of law.

GOOD: In Smith, the court ruled that Smith had been deprived of property without due process of law.

7. Commas Before Quotations

Don't put a comma before a quotation if the quotation flows normally in the sentence—i.e., if the sentence would make sense without the quotation marks.

BAD: The court found that Smith had been, "lying in wait for Jones."

GOOD: The court found that Smith had been "lying in wait for Jones."

If the quotation does not flow normally, then use a comma and capitalize the first word of the quotation:

BAD: The court explained "The facts show that Smith had been lying in wait for Jones."

GOOD: The court explained, "The facts show that Smith had been lying in wait for Jones."

8.   Headings at the Bottom of a Page

When you check your memo for the last time before handing it in, you'll often notice that a section heading (like "Facts" or "Applicable Statutes" or "Discussion"), or a subheading within the Discussion Section, is the last line on a page. This looks bad, so just move it to the next page.

9.   Latin Phrases

As I mentioned in the chapter on clear sentences, you should never use Latin phrases in your writing. But it's useful to know what they mean when you see them in your research. You can learn these as you encounter them, but just in case you'll find it helpful, I've listed eight of the most common ones here.

e.g.	for example
i.e.	that is
viz.	namely
et al.	and others
inter alia	among other things
ipso facto	by that fact alone
res ipsa loquitur	the thing speaks for itself
in camera	in private with a judge rather than in open court

10. What Courts Do

You'll often start a sentence with the subject "the court," and you'll therefore need verbs to follow it. So it's useful to keep the following list in mind:

a) A court *does*:

"hold" (but be careful because a holding is narrow)

"rule"

"explain"

"reason"

"deem"

b) A court *does not*:

"argue"

c) A court "finds" *only facts*, not points of law.[15]

Incorrect: The court found that Smith was guilty.

Correct: The court found that the police had not planted the cocaine, so it ruled against Smith.

[15] Ordinarily, juries decide matters of fact whereas judges decide matters of law. In some cases there is no jury, so the judge decides both.

11.   Some Points About Citations

a) Full Citations

As you'll learn in the chapter on *The Bluebook*, you're permitted to use an abbreviated citation form after the first time you've cited a source. But you should always revert to the full citation whenever you cite something for the first time *in a new section of the memo* (e.g., the Facts, or the Discussion). If the Discussion is long, then I'd repeat this practice in every new subheading. Remember that the reader will often flip to one section or another without reading the whole memo.

b) Use Correct Abbreviations in Case Names

I mention this point because it's often neglected. *The Bluebook* requires you to abbreviate words in the names of cases, and it explains how to do so in Table 6.

c) Block Quotations

The citation goes outside the block, as demonstrated in this hypothetical example:

> The court emphasized that Mary's lamb was little.
>
> > Mary had a little lamb, little lamb, little lamb. Mary had a little lamb. Her fleece was white as snow. Mary had a little lamb, little lamb, little lamb. Mary had a little lamb. Her fleece was white as snow. Mary had a little lamb, little lamb, little lamb. Mary had a little lamb. Her fleece was white as snow.

Smith v. Jones, 212 U.S. 576, 577 (1902).

12. Hyphens and Dashes

Everyone makes a mess of hyphens and dashes. Just so you know, here's how they should be.

a) The Hyphen

- *What it is*: -

- *When to use it*: to connect the parts of a two-word adjective

Example

He has a rear-projection television set.

b) The En–Dash

- *What it is*: –

- *When to use it*: to separate times

Example

2:25–3:50 p.m.

c) The Em–Dash

- *What it is*: —

- *When to use it*: to separate a dependent clause within a sentence, as an alternative to commas or parentheses

Example

Jim—a plumber—joined us for dinner.

d) How to Make Hyphens and Dashes

To make a hyphen, simply use the hyphen key on your keyboard. To make an en-dash or an em-dash, go to "Insert," then "Symbol," then "Special Characters" on Microsoft Word.

II. Cases

When you do research to find an answer, you'll have to read cases—usually on the online databases of Lexis and Westlaw. Here are a few things you might want to keep in mind.

A. Which Court?

You need to learn which court decided a case in order to know how much the case will matter to the court deciding your case. To find out, look at the top of the opinion, either just above or just below (it varies) the names of the parties ("Smith v. Jones"). There you'll see the name of the court, or at least an abbreviation of the name.

Remember that there are six main possibilities. The court could be one of the three levels of federal court: (1) U.S. Supreme Court; (2) U.S. Court of Appeals; (3) U.S. District Court. Or it could be one of the (usually) three levels of state court: (1) state highest court; (2) state appeals court; (3) state trial court. You should be able to tell from the abbreviation which of these six levels the court represents and which jurisdiction (which state, or which federal circuit) it belongs to. Remember that the telltale sign that a court is federal rather than state is the label "U.S."

B. Date of Decision

Just below the names of the parties and the court, the opinion will tell you the date on which the case was decided. If it lists multiple dates (e.g., when the case was argued, etc.), then remember that the important one for your purposes is the date of decision. When you cite a case and provide the year, that's the year you're referring to.

C. Which Part is the Opinion?

When you read a case on Lexis or Westlaw, there's often a lot of text summarizing the case, before the opinion starts. It's essential for you to understand that this material *isn't the opinion* and therefore *cannot be cited or quoted*. That material is written by people who work at Lexis or Westlaw, and if you rely on it, you do so at your own risk because there's no guarantee that those people correctly understood the opinion. You can reliably learn what an opinion says only by reading it yourself.

But how do you know where the summary material ends and the opinion begins? The tip-off is the name of the judge who authored the opinion: *The opinion starts immediately after the words "Smith, Judge" or "Williams, J." or "Jones, Circuit Judge," or "Johnson, District Judge," etc.*

Anything written above (before) the start of the opinion doesn't count. Some people find the summaries useful and others don't, but they're no substitute for reading the opinion itself.

D.   Finding What's Relevant

Very often, your search will turn up a case that covers many points of law, only one of which is relevant to your topic. Although you want to get a sense of what's going on in the case, you don't want to waste your time delving into all the irrelevant issues.

Sometimes you can skip to your issue by looking for your search terms, as described in the chapter on research. When this fails, you'll just have to skim through the opinion to try to find your issue. It won't take long for you to develop this skill; but at the beginning, you might find yourself slogging through material that doesn't matter in order to figure out what does. It can be frustrating, but it's valuable to your progress as a lawyer.

E.   Understanding the Opinion

Some judges write clear, easy-to-read opinions, whereas others don't. When you have trouble understanding an opinion, slow down and try to read carefully enough to identify the source of the confusion. In many cases the problem is simply that the opinion uses words you've never encountered before. If you have the patience to look up all of those words (e.g., in *Black's Law Dictionary* or <http://www.dictionary.com>), then you'll solve the immediate problem and will also help yourself read cases faster and more easily in the future.

F.   Holding vs. Dicta

If a court says something in its opinion that isn't necessary to the result—if it expresses a view about something, but the result of the case would be the same regardless whether the court had taken that view—then that view is a "dictum."

Unlike a "holding," *a dictum is never binding authority* even if it comes from a higher court in the same jurisdiction. A state trial court is thus not required to follow a dictum from the supreme court of its own state. That said, dicta constitute persuasive authority, and lower courts in the same jurisdiction typically treat such dicta with respect.

It's often difficult to find the line between what constitutes a dictum and what constitutes a holding, and sometimes there simply isn't a clear answer.

III.   Statutes

As explained in the chapter on the legal system, there are four sources of law in the United States: constitutions, statutes, regulations, and cases. Although constitutions are the highest law, their provisions are usually so general that they don't come up in everyday legal work too frequently. Regulations are very important and drastically underemphasized in law school, but they apply to only the subset of cases involving the law of administrative agencies within the executive branch.

Ideally, the typical law school curriculum would give students a healthy exposure to all four sources of law, with a heavy emphasis on statutes and cases because those apply most often to legal practice. Instead, the typical curriculum focuses almost entirely on cases. You could graduate from many good law schools without knowing what a statute is.

That's unfortunate, and I can't remedy it here. But at least I can tell you a little bit about statutes so they won't seem so foreign when you encounter them in your legal job.

Recall that a statute is a law enacted by a legislature, state or federal. Statutes always trump common law (the law created by courts) and are in turn trumped only by the state or federal constitution.

A.   Legislative History

When a court applies a statute to the facts of a case, it almost invariably must resolve a dispute about what the statute means. It usually begins that task by considering the text of the statute, including any definitions the statute gives for its own terms. If the statute doesn't define those terms, then the court might look up the definitions in an authoritative dictionary like *Webster's Third New International Dictionary*, *The Oxford English Dictionary*, or *Black's Law Dictionary*.

But sometimes the text isn't enough to clarify the statute's meaning, so courts look at the "legislative history" to find clues about what the legislators intended. Legislative history is everything that members of the legislature (senators and members of the house of representatives) said or wrote about a bill while they were drafting it and revising it. It gives us valuable clues about what the drafters intended the words to mean.

To understand how you can look up the legislative history of a statute, you need to know how a statute is created. First, a senator or representative writes a bill and *introduces* it to the legislative body that she's in (either the senate or the house). Let's say a senator introduced the bill. It is then *numbered*—e.g., "S. 498" ("S." means it originated in the senate; had it originated in the house of representatives, it would have a number like "H.R. 498"). After the bill is numbered, it is sent to a *committee* of senators (again, had it been introduced in the house, it would have gone to a committee of house members).

The committee will discuss the bill and might change it. Then, the committee will vote on whether to pass the bill along to the full senate. If the committee votes not to do so, then the bill dies. If the committee does vote to pass the bill along, then it prepares a *committee report* that explains what it thinks the text of the bill means. The full senate will then *debate* the bill and finally will *vote* on whether to pass it.

If the senate passes the bill, then the house of representatives takes it up. (If the bill had originated in the house, then it would move to the senate after being passed in the house.) The bill goes to a committee of house members, who might change it. If the house committee votes to approve the bill, then it might write its own *committee report*. The entire house of representatives then *debates* the bill and *votes* on it. Let's say they vote to pass it.

If the bill that passed the senate is meaningfully different from the one that passed the house, then there is a *conference committee* meeting between members of the senate and house. If this new committee reaches an agreement, it produces a *conference report* explaining what the revised bill means. The revised bill then must be passed by both the senate and the house.

If the President or the governor (depending on whether the bill was moving through the federal legislature or a state legislature) signs the bill that both houses of the legislature passed, then the bill becomes a *statute* and is binding law.

When you do research to look up the legislative history of a statute, there are two main types of documents that matter. The first and most important is a committee report. Ideally, you'll have a conference committee report (which matters the most), or if not, then at least a senate and/or house committee report. The second type of document is a set of statements of senators or house members on the floor of the Congress during the debates about the bill. In the federal legislature, these statements are collected in something called the "Congressional Record."

Researching legislative history can be difficult, and you shouldn't hesitate to ask a librarian for help in finding committee reports and statements of legislators.

B. Statutes on Lexis and Westlaw

Let's say you need to look up the federal statute that makes it a crime to own a machinegun, and you have the citation (18 U.S.C. § 922(*o*)). It's tempting just to type that citation into "Find by Citation" on Westlaw or "Get a Document" and "Get by Citation" on Lexis. But if you do that and nothing else, you'll miss a lot.

Using "Find" for statutes will show you the particular section you're looking for (in this case, § 922), but it won't show you where that section fits into the larger statutory scheme. That's crucial because a related section might be necessary to understand your section, and you won't even be aware that the related section exists if you simply search directly for your section.

Let me walk you through a different way to look up a statute—using the *Table of Contents* of the state or federal code. In Westlaw, you'd click on the database directory "View Westlaw Directory," then "U.S. Federal Materials," then "Statutes," then "United States Code Annotated (U.S.C.A.)" (USCA), then *instead of typing in search terms, click on* "Table of Contents" (at the top). You know from the citation (18 U.S.C. § 922(*o*)) that you're looking for Title 18, so click the plus sign next to that Title.

Then click the plus sign next to "Part I: Crimes," because you're dealing with a crime. It'll then be clear that what you want is "Chapter 44: Firearms." After clicking that plus sign, you'll see "§ 922: Unlawful Acts." But you'll also see "§ 921: Definitions." *You would have missed § 921 if you'd just typed your citation into* "Find by Citation."

On Lexis, you would have clicked on "Federal Legal—U.S.," then "USCS—United States Code Service: Code, Const, Rules, Conventions & Public Laws," then the plus sign next to Title 18, and so on.

As it turns out, section 922(*o*) says that "it shall be unlawful for any person to transfer or possess a machinegun," and section 921 defines what constitutes a machinegun. Both are probably things your reader wants to know.

It's valuable to follow the steps above to get a feel for the Table of Contents, but after you've done that once, there's a shortcut you can use in the future. *You can type the statute's citation into "Find" or "Get by Citation," then when the statute appears, click on "TOC" (Lexis, top left corner) or "Table of Contents" (Westlaw, toolbar on left).*

C. Cases Interpret Statutes

As a parting thought on statutes, I'd like to note a common and dangerous mistake that is easily avoided. Lawyers often read a statute and assume their question is answered by the plain text of the law. But courts interpret statutes in surprising ways, so *the easiest and best way to learn how a court will interpret a statute is to see how the statute has been interpreted by other courts (or, better yet, by that court itself).* Looking up the text and (perhaps) the legislative history are the first things you should do, but not the last.

Chapter 6

GUIDE TO *THE BLUEBOOK*

As you know, you write a legal memo to answer a question that your reader asked. And the answer comes from your research—from the statutes, cases, and other sources you find. When you convey that answer in your memo, you need to tell the reader which sources you relied on, and you need to do so in a way that enables the reader to look up those sources herself.

If it were up to me, a lawyer wouldn't be expected to cite each source the same way every other lawyer cites it. There's more than one way to give the reader all the relevant information, and I don't see why it's necessary for everyone to fit the information into a uniform system. Indeed, I think it wastes time for all lawyers to have to learn the intricacies of a 400–page book devoted to creating such a system.

But it's not up to me. Many readers will expect you to cite legal sources in the form given by *The Bluebook: A Uniform System of Citation*. The book contains hundreds if not thousands of rules, sub-rules, examples, and tables in an effort to enable a writer to cite any possible source precisely the same way as all other writers cite it.

I've already spent hundreds of hours learning and using these rules, but you haven't, so maybe I can save you a bit of time. In this chapter, I summarize some of the most important rules in a way that will, I hope, make them easier to understand than they'd be if you got them from *The Bluebook* itself. You'll still need to own *The Bluebook* and refer to it constantly, but at least it should be a bit less daunting after my summary.

I.   This Guide and *The Bluebook*

In this chapter, my goal isn't to explain everything in *The Bluebook*—far from it. The chapter is a guide or supplement, not a replacement. Let me explain briefly its modest aims.

The Bluebook has been around for a long time, and at the time my book is published, the most recent edition is the 18th. If you find yourself using a newer edition than that, you'll need to be all the more vigilant in making sure that my guide doesn't lead you astray. Chances are good that most of what I write here will still apply because I'm covering only the most widely applicable rules (those least likely to change dramatically), but you never know.

The Bluebook contains eight main parts. Three of them—the Table of Contents, the Introduction, and the Index—help you find things in the rest of the book. A fourth—the panels inside the front and back covers—shows you examples of how to cite most sources. A fifth—the tables on the blue-rimmed pages in the back—is a reference where you can look up abbreviations and the names of courts and statutory codes for virtually every U.S. jurisdiction, along with many foreign jurisdictions and international organizations. A sixth—the Bluepages in the front—summarizes the main rules and tells you how to convert them to the form used by practitioners. This sixth part needs some explanation.

The Bluebook isn't written primarily for lawyers but for student-run law reviews. The rules on the white pages in the main body of the book are for the law reviews. But they can and should be used by practitioners (regular lawyers) too, with slight modifications. The blue pages in the front demonstrate those modifications, which are also illustrated by comparing the panels inside the front cover (law review sample citations) to those inside the back cover (practitioners' sample citations).

Finally, the most important parts of the book are the rules themselves, which fall into two categories. First, there are rules 1–9. These apply to all of your writing and citations, so they come up most often. Second, there are rules 10–21, which go into the gory details of how to cite every imaginable case, statute, regulation, book, or article, plus many unimaginable ones.

I know no way to simplify rules 10–21. You just need to use them as references, in tandem with the tables in the back, to show yourself how to cite each source that comes up in your memo. The best I can do is give a few examples of proper citations for the main sources you're likely to encounter.

After those examples, this chapter gives a summary of rules 1–9. Even this summary, though it strives to be relatively thorough, is necessarily incomplete. I'm trying to express the same rules *The Bluebook* sets out, but with explanations that are somewhat less exhaustive and easier to understand. Although I don't use the identical words or examples of *The Bluebook* except where indicated, I do use similar examples and explanations. Obviously, I'm not trying to take credit for the points contained in the very source for which I'm writing a guide. The similarities are necessary because the nature of my project is to convey the same information in a somewhat more accessible way.

It should thus be clear that the best way to insure accuracy is always to use *The Bluebook* itself, not this guide, as your ultimate reference.

II. The Index

There will be many times when you want to look something up in *The Bluebook*, and fortunately there's a simple way to find most things—the incredibly thorough Index in the back of the book (pages 381–415 of the 18th edition). If, for example, you wanted to look up the rules governing the ellipsis, you'd just look up "ellipsis" in the Index and go to the corresponding page. That's usually the fastest and most efficient way to find what you need.

III. Differences Between Law Review Form and Practitioners' Form

As noted above, the main body of *The Bluebook* dictates the citation form for law reviews, which is slightly different from the form you're expected to use as a lawyer. *The main difference is that case names are not underlined (or italicized) in law review footnotes, whereas they are in the memos you'll write.* The front section called The Bluepages (pp. 3–43 of the 18th edition) shows every adjustment relevant to memo-writing, but the key is simply to know about case names and to know that the fancy typeface convention of LARGE AND SMALL CAPITALS is generally replaced with simple underlining in a memo. Italics and underlining are interchangeable, and either is fine if used consistently. I use underlining here because it's still more common than italics for practitioners.

LAW REVIEW FOOTNOTE: *See* Brown v. Bd. of Educ., 347 U.S. 483, 486 (1954)

MEMO: <u>See</u> <u>Brown v. Bd. of Educ.</u>, 347 U.S. 483, 486 (1954)

LAW REVIEW FOOTNOTE: JOHN RAWLS, A THEORY OF JUSTICE 54 (1971)

MEMO: John Rawls, <u>A Theory of Justice</u> 54 (1971)

IV. Some Examples of Common Citations

The following examples are an exceedingly rough and incomplete introduction to some basic citation forms. I include them only to give you a sense of what citations look like.

A. Cases

When a court decides a case, its opinion gets published in a book so everyone can look it up. These books are called "reporters" because they merely report the courts' decisions (in chronological order). Each of the three levels of federal court has its own reporter—its own set of books containing the opinions of all courts at that level. The decisions of the U.S. Supreme Court are published in a book called "U.S."; the decisions of the federal courts of appeals are published in a book called "F." (and more recent cases are in "F.2d" or "F.3d"); and the decisions of the federal district courts are published in a book called "F. Supp." (and more recent cases are in "F. Supp. 2d"). State cases are published in their own reporters.

As you might imagine, it's not possible to fit every U.S. Supreme Court opinion in history into one volume of a book. So the reporter is published in hundreds of volumes. When you cite a case, you tell the reader where it's published by listing the *volume number*, then the *reporter* (e.g., "U.S." or

"F." or "F. Supp." or a state reporter), then the page number of the relevant volume. The case Brown v. Board of Education appears in volume 347 of the U.S. Reports, and it *starts* on page 483 of that volume. If you made reference to a point found on page 486 of that volume (within the Brown opinion), you'd cite it like this:

> Brown v. Bd. of Educ., 347 U.S. 483, 486 (1954)

Thus, the basic citation form for a case is:

> Party 1 v. Party 2, [Volume] [Reporter] [First Page], [Specific Pages] ([Court] [Year])

The "year" is the year in which the case was decided. In U.S. Supreme Court cases, only the year appears in the parenthetical at the end. But for all other courts, you designate the court in the parenthetical, too.

> Smith v. Jones, 111 F.3d 456, 474 (11th Cir. 1997).[16]

To find out how to abbreviate the name of a court or a reporter, use Table 1 in the back of *The Bluebook* (pp. 193–242 of the 18th edition). The Table starts with each federal court, then covers all state courts in alphabetical order by state.

---

[16] Most of the cases and other sources that I use as examples in this chapter, starting with this one, are fictional.

B. Statutes

Statutes are published in books, too, but they're usually not organized by volume numbers and page numbers. The books are called *codes*, and they're divided into *titles* and *sections*. Federal statutes are part of the U.S. Code, which is abbreviated "U.S.C." So a federal statute would be cited like this:

19 U.S.C. § 27 (2000).

Note that the year *doesn't refer to when the statute was enacted*, but rather to *when the code was published*. Thus, the basic citation form for a statute is:

[Title] [Code] [Section] ([Year])

Table 1 in the back of *The Bluebook* will show you how to abbreviate each state's statutory code.

C. Law Review Articles

Law review articles are published in books that are organized, like case reporters, by volumes and pages. Here's how you'd cite an article that appears in volume 60 of the Michigan Law Review and that starts on page 841 of that volume:

Philip Jackson, Paradoxes of Federal Income Taxation, 60 Mich. L. Rev. 841, 856 (1962).

Table 13 in the back of *The Bluebook* (pp. 349–72 of the 18th edition) shows you how to abbreviate the name of each law review.

V. Rules 1–9

A. Rule 1: Citations

The core idea behind *The Bluebook* is that when you make a statement about what the law is, you should back up that statement by citing something (a case, a statute, a book, etc.) that supports it. You wouldn't write merely this sentence:

> American law prohibits segregation in schools.

Instead, you'd add a citation like this one:

> American law prohibits segregation in schools. See Brown v. Bd. of Educ., 347 U.S. 483 (1954).

The word "See" in the example is called an "introductory signal" because it introduces the source (the authority you're citing, in this case Brown v. Bd. of Educ.) and signals how the source relates to your sentence. You might think that "see" would be the only signal; but believe it or not, there are four *categories* of signal, the first of which alone contains *six* different signals. Welcome to the world of legal citation.

1. The Four Categories of Signal

Typically, you cite a source that supports what you've just written—one that says what you've said. But you could also cite a source that provides general background on the topic, or even one that contradicts your statement (e.g., to make the reader aware of the opposing view). Another option would be to cite two sources whose comparison sheds light on your point. Thus, the four categories of signal are: (1) Support, (2) Comparison, (3) Contradiction, and (4) Background.

Each of these four categories contains its own set of signals, as follows.

a) The Support Category

There are six signals that indicate support: no signal, e.g., accord, see, see also, and cf.

i) no signal

When you cite a source with no signal, it looks like this:

> American law prohibits segregation in schools. Brown v. Bd. of Educ., 347 U.S. 483 (1954).

Using no signal means that the source you're citing *states the point* for which you're citing it, or stands directly for that point. You'd also use no signal whenever you *quote* from—or *name*—the cited source in the sentence before the citation.

ii) e.g.,

This signal means "for example" and can be used in combination with other signals like no signal or see.

American law prohibits segregation in schools. E.g., Brown v. Bd. of Educ., 347 U.S. 483 (1954).

or

American law prohibits segregation in schools. See, e.g., Brown v. Bd. of Educ., 347 U.S. 483 (1954).

Notice that the first letter of a signal is *capitalized only if it starts a sentence*. Notice also that both periods in e.g. are underlined, but the *comma following* e.g. *is not underlined*. Finally, the *comma and space between* see *and* e.g. *are underlined*.

iii) accord

Use this signal when your sentence refers to one case, and you cite not only that case but also other sources that say precisely the same thing.

As the Court held in Brown, American law prohibits segregation in schools. Brown v. Bd. of Educ., 347 U.S. 483 (1954); accord Smith v. Jones, 111 F.3d 456 (11th Cir. 1997).

Once again, notice that accord isn't capitalized here because it isn't the first word of a sentence.

iv) see

Whereas no signal means that the source states your point or stands directly for it, see means that your point "obviously follows from" the cited source—that "an inferential step" is required.

Let's imagine that the Idaho Supreme Court has held, in a case called <u>Penny v. Moore</u>, that anyone who has lived in Idaho for at least four years is an Idaho citizen. You're writing a memo on a related issue. If you write the first sentence below, then you'd use no signal; but if you write the second sentence below, then you'd use <u>see</u>.

> If a person has lived in Idaho for four years or more, then she is a citizen of Idaho. <u>Penny v. Moore</u>, 261 P.3d 989, 993 (Idaho 2002).

> but

> Jane is an Idaho citizen because she has lived in Idaho for four years. <u>See</u> <u>Penny v. Moore</u>, 261 P.3d 989, 993 (Idaho 2002).

v) <u>see also</u>

The Bluebook doesn't give an entirely satisfactory explanation of this signal, but most writers use it when they've already cited other authorities that strongly support a proposition and are now citing authorities that support the proposition a bit less strongly.

> As the Court held in <u>Brown</u>, American law prohibits segregation in schools. <u>Brown v. Bd. of Educ.</u>, 347 U.S. 483 (1954); <u>see also</u> <u>Smith v. Jones</u>, 111 F.3d 456 (11th Cir. 1997).

Note that the space between <u>see</u> and <u>also</u> *is underlined*.

vi) <u>cf.</u>

This is the weakest support signal, and it means that the source you're citing says something different from your sentence but analogous to it.

> American law prohibits segregation in schools. <u>Brown v. Bd. of Educ.</u>, 347 U.S. 483 (1954); <u>cf. Smith v. Jones</u>, 111 F.3d 456 (11th Cir. 1997).

Note that this signal falls under the first category (*support*) rather than the second (*comparison*) even though "cf." literally means "compare." Note also that the period after <u>cf.</u> should be *underlined*.

b) *The Comparison Category*

This category has only one signal, and it's rarely used:

<u>compare</u> X <u>with</u> Y

You use this signal when the comparison between the two sources will support or demonstrate your point.

> American law prohibits segregation in schools. <u>Compare Brown v. Bd. of Educ.</u>, 347 U.S. 483 (1954) <u>with</u> <u>Smith v. Jones</u>, 111 F.3d 456 (11th Cir. 1997).

Both <u>compare</u> and <u>with</u> should be underlined.

c) *The Contradiction Category*

This category has three signals: <u>contra</u>, <u>but see</u>, and <u>but cf.</u> Remember that <u>e.g.</u> can be used with any signal, including these.

i) contra

This is the negative version of no signal, indicating that the cited authority directly contradicts what you've written.

> American law permits segregation in schools. Contra Brown v. Bd. of Educ., 347 U.S. 483 (1954).

ii) but see

This is the negative version of see, indicating that the cited authority contradicts what you've written via an inferential step.

> Jane is not an Idaho citizen even though she has lived in Idaho for four years. But see Penny v. Moore, 261 P.3d 989, 993 (Idaho 2002).

The space between but and see is underlined.

iii) but cf.

This is the negative version of cf.

d) The Background Category

There's one signal in this category:

see generally

You use see generally when the source doesn't come down in favor of, or against, your point but rather provides background information about the subject. Don't get confused by the fact that this signal starts with the word "see"; *it's not in the support category*.

2. Putting Sources in Order

You'll often find yourself citing more than one source after your sentence. What order do you put the sources in? Here are the rules.

a) Order of Signals

First, you separate the citations by category of signal. All the support signals go first, then the comparison signals, then the contradiction signals, and finally the background signals.

Within each category, put the signals in the order listed above. For example, "no signal" would precede see, which would in turn precede cf.

All citations within one signal category are separated by semicolons. Citations from different categories are separated by periods.

> Mary had a little lamb. Smith v. Jones, 459 F.3d 761, 764 (11th Cir. 2001); see also Williams v. Baker, 382 F. Supp. 2d 290, 296 (E.D.N.Y. 1998); Cabot v. Cook, 435 N.E.2d 585, 598–99 (Ind. 2002); cf., e.g., Adams v. Price, 548 U.S. 366, 381 (2003) (holding that Susie, Mary's sister, had a little lamb). But cf. Halama v. Maartens, 461 U.S. 902, 903–04 (1980) (noting that Mary's brother Mike did not have a little lamb). See generally Marquez v. Kane, 411 S.W.2d 501, 532–44 (Tenn. Ct.

App. 1968) (discussing the origins
of lamb ownership in America).

This example, though dense, illustrates a lot. If you
go through it carefully, you'll see how many of the
rules work.

The first citation, to <u>Smith v. Jones</u>, uses no
signal. That comes first because it's in the support
category and is the first type of signal in that
category.

That first citation is followed by a semicolon,
because the next signal (<u>see also</u>) is in the support
category, too. Two cases (<u>Williams v. Baker</u> and
<u>Cabot v. Cook</u>) are cited within the <u>see also</u> signal,
separated by a semicolon. Next comes <u>cf.</u> (another
support signal), which in this case is followed by <u>e.g.</u>

There's a period after the <u>cf.</u> citation (<u>Adams v.
Price</u>) and immediately preceding the <u>but cf.</u> citation. That's because <u>but cf.</u> is in a different *category*
of signal (the contradiction category) from the signals that went before (which were all support signals). There's also a period between the <u>but cf.</u>
citation and the <u>see generally</u> citation, which is in
the background category.

b) *Order of Authorities Within Each Sig-nal*

Look again at the dense example above (the
"Mary had a little lamb" paragraph). Within the
<u>see also</u> signal, two cases are cited: <u>Williams v.
Baker</u> and <u>Cabot v. Cook</u>. How do you decide which
to put first?

111

The Bluebook gives a thorough list on pages 48–51 of the 18th edition (Rule 1.4) of the order of authorities within a signal. A quick summary is: (1) constitutions, (2) statutes, (3) treaties, (4) cases (federal, then state, then foreign; and highest to lowest level within those categories), (5) legislative materials, (6) administrative materials, (7) secondary sources (books, articles, etc.).

Williams v. Baker and Cabot v. Cook are both cases, so Williams goes first because it's a federal case (even though it's in the lowest level of federal court, whereas Cabot is in the highest level of state court).

3. Parentheticals

As you can see in the example above, it's often a good idea to use a parenthetical statement to explain what a source says.

The parenthetical must begin with a word ending in "ing" like "explaining" or "describing" or "noting," but there's one exception: If you're using the parenthetical to quote directly from the source, and your quote is a full sentence, then you don't introduce the quote with an "ing" word.

> But cf. Halama v. Maartens, 461 U.S. 902, 903–04 (1980) (noting that Mary's brother Mike did not have a little lamb).

> **or**

> But cf. Halama v. Maartens, 461 U.S. 902, 903–04 (1980) ("Mike owned no lamb.").

When you quote a full sentence, there's a period inside the parenthetical in addition to any punctuation outside it.

B. Rule 2: Typefaces (underlining)

You can tell from Rule 1 that it's not always easy to know what should be underlined. And this is made all the more difficult by the fact that the rules of *The Bluebook* use typeface conventions (italics and small capitals) that don't apply to practitioners' writing. Use the panel inside the back cover, and (even more important) the front blue pages to convert these typefaces to practitioners' form.

1. Punctuation

Underline only what comes within a citation, not punctuation immediately following a citation.

> See, e.g., id.

The comma between "see" and "e.g." is underlined, but the *comma after* "e.g." is *not* underlined because the citation ends with e.g. The *periods* in e.g. and id. *are* underlined.

2. Case Names Within Article Titles

If a case name appears in an article title, then underline every word of the article title *except for* the case name.

> Jim Friedman, Why Miranda Is Wrong, 99 Harv. L. Rev. 532, 597 (1986).

3. Typefaces in Your Sentences

Within your sentences, you should underline case names, as well as titles of publications (e.g., books or articles) and speeches.

> • In <u>Smith</u>, the court observed that Mary's lamb was white.

> • Sarah Johnson's article <u>Puzzles of the Commerce Clause</u> appears in the latest issue of the <u>Stanford Law Review</u>.

Notice that the comma after <u>Smith</u> and the period after <u>Stanford Law Review</u> are *not underlined* because the punctuation after the underlined source is never underlined.

C. Rule 3: Citing Parts of Sources

When you cite a source, you direct the reader not just to the case or book (or whatever), but also to the place within that case or book where the relevant point is made. You typically accomplish this by citing page numbers, but there are also other parts of sources that you might need to grapple with.

1. Volume Numbers

Not everyone writes books as short as this one. When a book is too long to fit into one bound volume, it must be published in two or more separate volumes. When you cite such a book, put before the author's name the number of the volume you're citing—as strange as this looks.

> 2 Jane Wilson, The Miracle of Federalism
> 408–09 (2d ed. 1986).

Articles usually appear in journals, and those journals are published in volumes. For articles, the volume number precedes the journal name. (This is similar to cases, where the volume number precedes the name of the "reporter"—the book where the case is published.)

> Philip Jackson, Paradoxes of Federal Income Taxation, 60 Mich. L. Rev. 841, 856 (1962).

2. Pages

Don't write "p." or "pp."—just the page number itself.

> Beth Harris, The Idea of Comity 268 (1997).

In the above example, you're directing the reader to page 268 of Harris's book. *With books, there's no comma before the page number.* However, you can use a comma and "at" if needed to avoid confusion:

> James Smith, Presidents of the United States from 1800 to 1900, at 45 (1987).
>
> Heather Jones, Physics and Law, at viii (1998).

Things are a bit different with articles:

> Philip Jackson, Paradoxes of Federal Income Taxation, 60 Mich. L. Rev. 841, 856 (1962).

Here, you're telling the reader that Jackson's article was published in volume 60 of the <u>Michigan Law Review</u>. The article begins on page 841, and on page 856 it makes the point for which you're citing it.

3. Multiple Pages

Repeat only the last two digits if more would be repetitive.

> Jim Friedman, <u>Why</u> Miranda <u>Is Wrong</u>, 99 Harv. L. Rev. 532, 587–99 (1986).

> **BUT**

> Jim Friedman, <u>Why</u> Miranda <u>Is Wrong</u>, 99 Harv. L. Rev. 532, 597–603 (1986).

If a hyphen would be ambiguous, then use the word "to."

> Catherine Jones, <u>Copyright Law</u> 7–21 to 7–23 (1997).

> Kelly Thompson & Richard Martin, <u>Business Organizations</u> ¶ 8.54, at 1–14 to 1–17 (3d ed. 1992).

Cite nonconsecutive pages by using commas.

> <u>Smith v. Jones</u>, 211 U.S. 451, 455, 498 (1904).

> <u>Smith v. Jones</u>, 211 U.S. 451, 455–57, 468, 498–502, 505 (1904).

4. Footnotes

When you cite a footnote within a source, you list the page where the footnote appears, then the footnote number preceded by "n."

> Philip Jackson, Paradoxes of Federal Income Taxation, 60 Mich. L. Rev. 841, 856 n.97 (1962).

Notice that there's *no space between* "n." and the number.

If you want to cite both the text and the footnote that appears on that page (as opposed to just the footnote), then use an ampersand.

> Philip Jackson, Paradoxes of Federal Income Taxation, 60 Mich. L. Rev. 841, 856 & n.97 (1962).

5. Multiple Footnotes

If you're citing more than one footnote, just use "nn." for multiple *consecutive* footnotes.

> Philip Jackson, Paradoxes of Federal Income Taxation, 60 Mich. L. Rev. 841, 856 nn.115–19 (1962).

Use "nn." *and* an ampersand if the cited footnotes are *nonconsecutive*.

> Philip Jackson, Paradoxes of Federal Income Taxation, 60 Mich. L. Rev. 841, 856 nn.115 & 119 (1962).

> Philip Jackson, Paradoxes of Federal Income Taxation, 60 Mich. L. Rev. 841, 856 nn.115–16 & 119 (1962).

> Philip Jackson, Paradoxes of Federal Income Taxation, 60 Mich. L. Rev. 841, 856 nn.115–19, 860–61 nn. 123 & 125–26, 870 nn.159–61, 163 & 165–66 (1962).

6.   Sections and Paragraphs

When a source is divided into sections or paragraphs rather than pages, use these symbols: § (section) and ¶ (paragraph).

19 U.S.C. § 27 (2000).

Laura Taylor, <u>Bankruptcy</u> ¶ 87.34 (1991).

Never use "at" before a section or paragraph symbol.

RIGHT: <u>Id.</u> § 5.

WRONG: <u>Id.</u> at § 5.

RIGHT: Johnson, <u>supra</u> n.5, ¶ 56.

WRONG: Johnson, <u>supra</u> n.5, at ¶ 56.

7.   Multiple Sections and Paragraphs

When you cite more than one section or paragraph, use two symbols: §§ or ¶¶.

19 U.S.C. §§ 27–29 (2000).

Unlike multiple pages, multiple sections and paragraphs must be cited in their entirety—*not just the last two digits*.

RIGHT: 19 U.S.C. §§ 127–129 (2000).

WRONG: 19 U.S.C. §§ 127–29 (2000).

Use *one* symbol (§) to cite multiple subsections in the *same* section, *but* use *two* symbols (§§) to cite multiple subsections in *different* sections.

12 U.S.C. § 24(d)(3)–(e)(1) (2000).

BUT

28 U.S.C. §§ 24(d), 26(b) (2000).

8. Appendices, Comments, and Notes

Sometimes you need to cite the appendix of a book or article, or a comment or note within the book.

To cite an entire appendix, you'd do this:

> Jennifer Smith, <u>Rights and Duties</u>, 101 Yale L.J. 233 app. (1991).

To cite one page of the appendix, you'd do this:

> Jennifer Smith, <u>Rights and Duties</u>, 101 Yale L.J. 233 app. at 324 (1991).

Here's how you cite a comment:

> <u>Restatement (Second) of Contracts</u> § 47 cmt. b (1981).

And here's how you cite a note, as in a note of the Advisory Committee on a federal rule.

> <u>Fed. R. Civ. P.</u> 23(a)(1) advisory committee's note.

9. Internal Cross References

You can refer the reader to another part of your own memo by using the terms <u>supra</u> (above) and <u>infra</u> (below). Only use these terms in citations; in the text, always use English rather than Latin.

Internal cross-references (<u>supra</u> and <u>infra</u>) are the *only* times that you should use "p." or "pp."

See supra Part II.

Cf. infra pp. 5–9.

D. Rule 4: Short Citation Forms (id.)

After you've cited a case or other source, you don't always need to repeat the whole citation again. When you're referring to the *most recent* source you cited, you can use "id."

> Mary had a little lamb. Jones v. Smith, 510 U.S. 165, 166 (2000). Her fleece was white as snow. Id. at 167.

Don't repeat the page number after "id." if you're citing the same page again.

> Mary had a little lamb. Jones v. Smith, 510 U.S. 165, 166 (2000). Her fleece was white as snow. Id.

If you cite more than one source for a proposition, then you may *not* use id. in the next citation because it wouldn't be clear which citation you're referring to.

> **RIGHT:** Mary had a little lamb. Jones v. Smith, 510 U.S. 165, 166 (2000); Williams v. Baker, 505 U.S. 102, 102 (1998). Her fleece was white as snow. Williams, 505 U.S. at 167.

> **WRONG:** Mary had a little lamb. Jones v. Smith, 510 U.S. 165, 166 (2000); Williams v. Baker, 505 U.S. 102, 102 (1998). Her fleece was white as snow. Id. at 167.

However, explanatory parentheticals and subsequent history do *not* prevent you from using "id." even if the parentheticals don't apply to the "id." citation.

> Mary had a "'little lamb.'" Jones v. Smith, 510 U.S. 165, 166 (2000) (quoting Swan v. Lake, 405 U.S. 341, 348 (1980)). Her fleece was white as snow. Id. at 167.

> Mary had a little lamb. Branch v. Kelly, 236 F. Supp. 767, 773 (E.D. La. 1954), aff'd per curiam, 315 U.S. 120 (1955). Her fleece was white as snow. Id. at 774.

E.   Rule 5: Quotations

Here are the rules that show you what to do when you quote a source directly.

1.   To Indent or not to Indent?

If the quote is 49 words or less, then quote regularly within a sentence.

> The court explained that "the lamb possessed by Mary was little." Jones v. Smith, 510 U.S. 165, 166 (2000).

If the quote is 50 words or more, then put it in a "block" that's indented on the left and right, and don't use quotation marks at all.

The court explained that

> Mary had a little lamb, little lamb, little lamb. Mary had a little lamb.

> Her fleece was white as snow.
> Mary had a little lamb, little lamb,
> little lamb. Mary had a little lamb.
> Her fleece was white as snow.
> Mary had a little lamb, little lamb,
> little lamb. Mary had a little lamb.
> Her fleece was white as snow.

Smith v. Jones, 212 U.S. 576, 577 (1902).

2. Brackets

Use brackets to show any change you've made from the original material you're quoting, like capitalizing or lowercasing a letter, adding or changing a word or part of a word, or omitting the end of a word (shown by empty brackets after the word).

Let's imagine you're quoting a book that says, "On September 1, the panel decides to meet in several weeks to reconsider the committee's proposals. That meeting will be on September 22." If you're writing about only one of the proposals, you could alter the quote as follows:

> "[T]he panel decide[d] to meet in [three] weeks to reconsider the committee's proposal[]."

If you add underlining to a quotation, then use a parenthetical to alert the reader.

> "Mary had a little lamb." Smith v. Jones, 521 U.S. 670, 672 (2002) (emphasis added).

If you underline a word, but another word was underlined in the original, then describe what you've done:

"Her <u>fleece</u> was white as <u>snow</u>." <u>Id.</u> (second emphasis added).

3. Ellipses

You will often want to omit words from a quotation, and you do this with an ellipsis: three periods with one space before, in between, and after (space, period, space, period, space, period, space).

RIGHT: He said, "I am . . . free."

WRONG: He said, "I am ... free."

WRONG: He said, "I am...free."

If you're omitting words at the end of a sentence, then use four periods. *Put a space between the last quoted word and the first period.*

"Ask not what your country can do . . . ."

But if you're quoting more than one sentence, and you omit material at the *beginning* of one of the sentences other than the first sentence, then indicate that by using four periods *without putting a space between the last word of the previous sentence and the first period.* This might seem a bit technical, but it makes sense.

"Mary had a little lamb . . . . [F]leece was white as snow."

F. Rule 6: Abbreviations, Numerals, and Symbols

a) Spacing

In general, *do not put a space* between two *single* capital letters that are next to each other but separated by periods.

> N.W.
>
> S.D.N.Y.

Always put a space between a single capital and an abbreviation of *two or more letters*.

> F. Supp.
>
> D. Mass.
>
> S. Ct.
>
> Harv. L. Rev.

When you cite law reviews, put a space between two single capital letters if one of them refers to geography or to a university and the other is just an abbreviation of the word "law" in the term "law review" or "law journal."

> N.C. L. Rev. ("L" separated from "N.C."— North Carolina)
>
> B.U. L. Rev. ("L" separated from "B.U."— Boston University)
>
> Ga. St. U. L. Rev. ("L" separated from Georgia State University)
>
> Ind. L.J. ("L.J." put together; they abbreviate "Law Journal")

Numbers (even ordinal numbers like 2d or 3d or 4th) are considered single capital letters. Therefore, put no space between numbers and other single capitals.

> N.W.3d
>
> F.2d
>
> A.L.R.4th

However, there should be a space between numbers and longer abbreviations.

> Pa. 2d
>
> F. Supp. 3d
>
> Mich. App. 2d

Do *not* put a space between initials in personal names.

> J.T. Snow

b) *Periods*

Don't use periods when something is commonly referred to by its abbreviation in speech. Here are the examples *The Bluebook* gives at page 73 of the 18th edition:

> AARP, CBS, CIA, FCC, FDA, FEC, NAACP, NLRB

Use a period to abbreviate a word, unless you're directed to use an apostrophe by Table 6 of *The Bluebook*. Never combine a period with an apostrophe in the same abbreviation.

Acad.
Bd.

Int'l
Env't

c) Numbers

Spell out the numbers zero through ninety-nine, and use numerals (like 101) for all bigger numbers.

However, there are six exceptions:

1) Always spell out a number that begins a sentence.

2) Spell out round numbers like "hundred" and "thousand."

3) When you write out several numbers in a series and some are above ninety-nine whereas others aren't, then use numerals for all of them.

• The three groups took, respectively, 287, 6, and 78 prisoners.

4) Use numerals if the number contains a decimal point.

• 3.6

5) Use numerals for percentages or dollar amounts if you refer to them repeatedly.

6) Use numerals to express the numbers of sections or other subdivisions (like paragraphs).

Use commas to separate digits if a number contains
five (*not* four) or more digits.

> 1,678,564
>
> **BUT**
>
> 6572

d) Section (§) and Paragraph (¶) Symbols

Always spell out "section" and "paragraph" if
they begin a sentence.

In citations, use the symbols: § and ¶ .

You should also use the symbols in your regular
sentences when you refer to sections of the U.S.
Code or federal regulations.

For sections or paragraphs of anything else,
spell out the words in your regular sentences rather
than using the symbols.

Always put a space between the symbol and the
number.

> **RIGHT:** § 5
>
> **WRONG:** §5
>
> **RIGHT:** ¶ 18
>
> **WRONG:** ¶18

e) Dollar ($) and Percent (%) Symbols

Never begin a sentence with a symbol. Otherwise, use the symbol only when the numeral is
used.

Give me fifteen dollars.
Give me $125.

I want fifty percent.
I want 150%.
I want 3.6%.

Put no space between a number and its dollar or percent symbol. This is the opposite of the rule for section and paragraph symbols.

> **RIGHT:** $125
>
> **WRONG:** $ 125
>
> **RIGHT:** 150%
>
> **WRONG:** 150 %

G.   Rule 7: Stylistic Underlining

1.   Underlining for Added Emphasis

- I was <u>hungry</u>.

2.   Foreign Words

Underline foreign words *unless* they are commonly used in English or are Latin words commonly used in law. Here are some examples.[17]

> <u>maison</u>
> <u>aequam servare mentem</u>
>
> **but**

---

[17] These are taken directly from page 50 of the 17th edition of *The Bluebook*. Although the 17th edition is no longer the most recent, these particular examples remain consistent with the rules of the 18th edition.

gestalt
i.e.
e.g.
quid pro quo
res judicata

3.　I̲d̲. and E.g.

Always underline "i̲d̲." You should underline "e.g." only when it's used as an introductory signal.

H.　Rule 8: Capitalization

1.　Headings and Titles

In headings and titles, capitalize:

(1) the first word,

(2) the first word right after a colon, and

(3) every other word except words *no longer than four letters* that are *articles, conjunctions,* or *prepositions.*

A̲ ̲R̲o̲o̲m̲ ̲w̲i̲t̲h̲ ̲a̲ ̲V̲i̲e̲w̲

A̲ ̲R̲o̲o̲m̲ ̲W̲i̲t̲h̲o̲u̲t̲ ̲a̲ ̲V̲i̲e̲w̲

P̲r̲o̲c̲e̲d̲u̲r̲a̲l̲ ̲F̲a̲i̲r̲n̲e̲s̲s̲:̲ ̲F̲o̲r̲ ̲t̲h̲e̲ ̲S̲a̲k̲e̲ ̲o̲f̲ J̲u̲s̲t̲i̲c̲e̲

D̲o̲ ̲Y̲o̲u̲ ̲T̲h̲i̲n̲k̲ ̲I̲t̲ ̲I̲s̲ ̲T̲i̲m̲e̲?̲

To learn whether a word is an article, conjunction, or preposition, look it up in the dictionary. Note that I don't follow this rule in my headings in this book.

2. Specific Legal Words

The Bluebook lists and discusses various words that come up frequently in law and that are capitalized only in certain instances. I refer you to this list on pages 76–78 of the 18th edition (Rule 8: Capitalization).

I. Rule 9: Judges

1. Supreme Court Justices are referred to as "Justice"

- Chief Justice Roberts *or* the Chief Justice
- Justice Souter

2. Other Judges are referred to as "Judge"

- Chief Judge Becker
- Judge Posner

Chapter 7

WRITING CHECKLIST

Here's a checklist that summarizes the most important writing suggestions I've made in the book. It might help to consult it just before you start writing a memo, and again (even more importantly) when you've completed a draft and want to revise.

I. The Four Most Important Things

A. Subject/Verb pairs

1.   Look at the *first words of each sentence* and make sure they feature a *short, concrete subject* (like "Smith" or "The court") followed *immediately* by a *verb*.

2.   After the start of the sentence, make sure that blocks of words are expressed with lots of subject/verb pairs.

B. Explain everything.

1.   *Assume zero knowledge*, especially in the *Introduction*, the *start of the Facts Section*, and the *start of the Discussion Section*.

2.   Throughout the Discussion Section, repeat the relevant facts as though the read-

er skipped the Facts Section. (This occurs during the "A" in IRAC.)

C. Replace every long or fancy word with a simpler equivalent.

D. Divide the Discussion Section into headings and sub-headings. Within each heading or sub-heading, use IRAC form.

1. *Discuss the most important precedent first, then the other precedents in order of importance.*

2. *Quote, don't paraphrase.*

II. Four Other Things to Keep in Mind

A. Make sure every sentence is relevant to the discussion where it is located, and that its relevance will be very clear to the reader. Check that each sentence follows logically from the one before it.

B. Keep the tone objective and dispassionate.

C. Check all quotations to avoid misquoting.

D. Do a final check for typographical and spelling errors, as well as for errors in *Bluebook* form.

INDEX

References are to pages.

GOVERNORS
State executive branch, 7

GRAMMAR RULES
Note on, 35–37
Subject/Verb Pairs, this index

HEADINGS
At bottom of page, moving, 82
Capitalization, Bluebook rules, 129
Structure of legal memo, 39–41

HOLDING
Dicta distinguished, 89

HOUSE OF REPRESENTATIVES
Legislative branch, 6

HYPHENS
Use of, 85–86

INDENTING
Quotations, 121–122

INDEX
Bluebook, 99

INDIVIDUAL RIGHTS
Generally, 10–11

INTERNAL CROSS–REFERENCES
Bluebook rules, 119–120

INTRODUCTION
Section of legal memo, 42–46

ITALICS
Case names, 100

JUDGES
Referring to, Bluebook rules, 130

JUDICIAL BRANCH
Generally, 7
Courts, this index
State government, 8

JURISDICTION
General and limited jurisdiction, 12–13

STATUTES AND LEGISLATION

STRUCTURE OF MEMO

STYLISTIC UNDERLINING

SUB–HEADINGS

SUBJECT/VERB PAIRS

SUPREMACY

†